COOL STUFF

Published by MQ Publications Limited
12 The Ivories, 6–8 Northampton Street, London N1 2HY
Tel: 020 7359 2244   Fax: 020 7359 1616
email: mail@mqpublications.com

Copyright © MQ Publications Limited 2002
All illustrations © Susie Lacome 1998

Series Editor: Ljiljana Ortolja-Baird
Editor: Jane Warren
Designer: Bet Ayer

A CIP catalogue record for this book is available
from the British Library
ISBN: 1-84072-463-3

First published in 1999 in hardback as Great Stuff (1-84072-069-7)
by MQ Publications Ltd, London.

Printed in China

COOL STUFF

100 fun projects for kids

susie lacome

MQP

contents

RAINY DAY

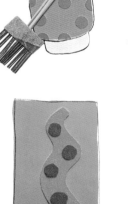

MAKE-BELIEVE

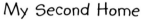

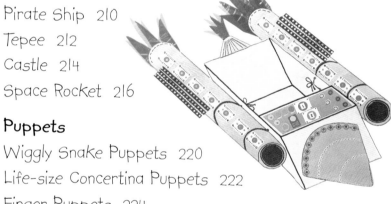

things you will need

Most of the projects in COOL STUFF can be made from things that can be found around the house, such as cardboard boxes, paper, fabric, sticky tape, glue, scissors and paints. Some projects use things found in nature, like leaves, twigs, sand, shells and pebbles. A few things for some projects will need to be bought, usually from a stationery shop, craft shop or hardware store.

GLUE

In COOL STUFF, unless it says so, glue always means PVA glue. PVA is excellent for sticking paper, card and cardboard and, although it goes on white, it dries clear.

Sometimes you will need to use waterproof glue – in which case use waterproof PVA – or fabric glue.

PAINT

In the same way, in this book, paint is always poster paint, unless acrylic or fabric paint is specifically listed. Poster paint is useful for painting card and paper, and is easily washed out of brushes when you are finished!

Acrylic paint sticks well to plastic surfaces, and it resists water. If you have no acrylic paint, a mixture of PVA glue and poster paint will often work just as well. In general, if you are going to paint a plastic or shiny surface, it is a good idea to sand it lightly before you begin, to give the paint a slightly rough surface to stick to.

Don't be put off if you can't find the exact colour of paint or paper or size of box mentioned - most of the projects can be adapted to whatever materials you have available, and the list of materials for each project should be seen as merely a guide. Improvise, make a plan, have a go – you will probably be thrilled with the results!

THINGS TO SAVE

Cardboard boxes - all sizes
Thin card - plain + coloured
Cardboard tubes - toilet rolls, fax paper,
        paper towel
Paper - plain, coloured, crepe, wrapping, tissue
Newspaper
Lids + tops - all sizes
Yoghurt, fromage frais pots
Egg cartons
Matchboxes
Plastic bottles - all sizes
Polystyrene or frozen pizza backing
Plastic milk containers
Glass jars
String, raffia, ribbon,
        wool scraps
Foam scraps
Fabric scraps
Hessian scraps
Empty cotton reels
Old socks, tights, clothes
Corks
Buttons + beads
Old rubber gloves
Plastic bags
Lolly sticks

THINGS TO FIND IN THE HOUSE

Pencil - with eraser tip
Ruler or tape measure
Felt tip pens - with ventilated caps
        for safety
Poster paints + paintbrushes
Scissors
Pinking shears
Tape - sticky, parcel, masking, insulation
Glue - PVA, fabric, waterproof, glue sticks
Craft knife
Bradawl
Silver foil

Pasta shapes
Dried lentils + beans
Cling film
Cotton wool
Plant canes
Plant ties
Needles - knitting, darning, sewing
Thread - sewing, embroidery
Pins
Safety pins
Clothes pegs
String, twine
Sandpaper

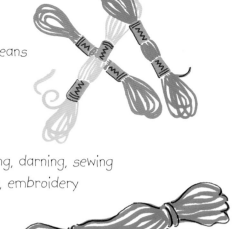

NATURAL THINGS TO COLLECT

Shells
Pebbles
Glass pieces worn smooth by weathering
Autumn leaves
Twigs, sticks - no sharp points
Straw

THINGS TO BUY

Acrylic or fabric paints
Raffia - different colours
Stickers - all types
Reinforcement rings
Gold foil or card
Fusible web
Double-sided tape
Tracing paper
Marker pens - silver, gold, waterproof
Paper clips - coloured
Pipe cleaners - coloured
Paper fasteners
Wire + garden wire
Magnets
Plastic cups
Plastic drinking straws
Balloons
Plant seeds, seedlings

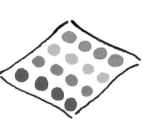

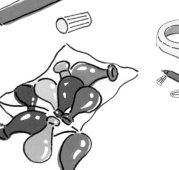

7

OUTDOOR garden

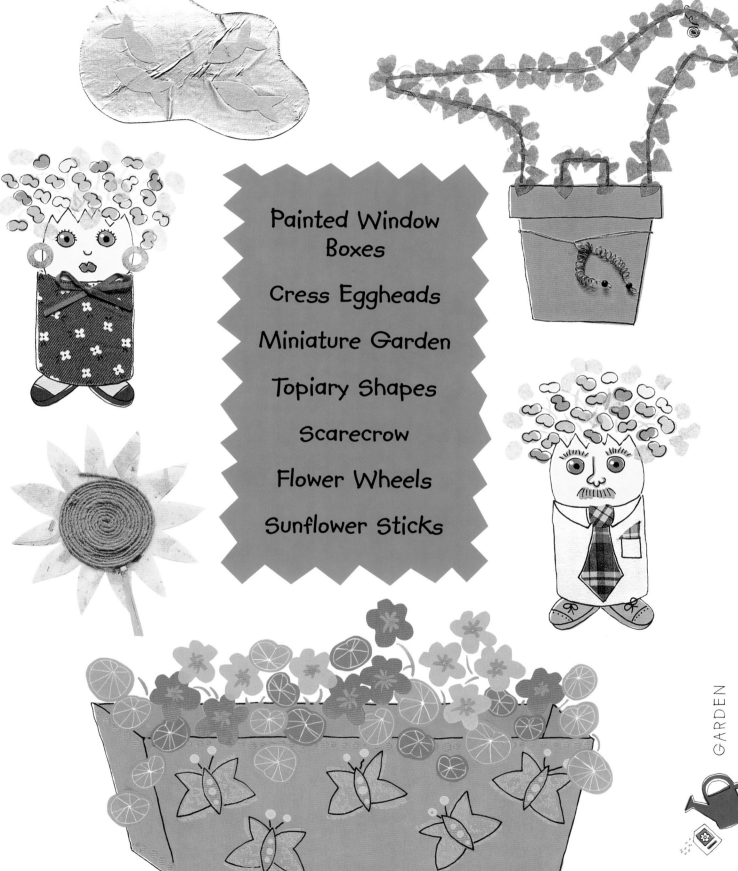

Painted Window
Boxes

Cress Eggheads

Miniature Garden

Topiary Shapes

Scarecrow

Flower Wheels

Sunflower Sticks

PAINTED WINDOW BOXES

you will need...

For the Bird Window Box

Plastic window box

Sandpaper

Acrylic paints

Paintbrushes

Masking tape

Thin card, a small
   sheet

Pencil, with eraser tip

Sponge

Scissors

Allow the paint to dry before carefully lifting and repositioning the stencil (see page 25l for hints).

Use bold, contrasting colours for the best results.

Paint the window boxes only on the outside.

These butterflies are done in 2 steps: first the wings and then the body, in a contrasting colour (see page 25l).

making a window box...

Bird

1 Lightly sand the window box so that the paint will stick to it. Mark a top and bottom border with masking tape. Paint the borders blue, and the centre yellow.

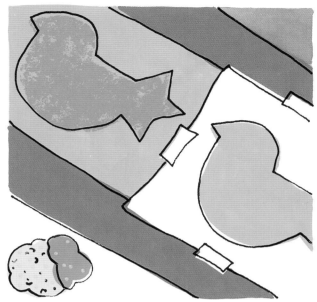

2 Cut a bird stencil from card (see page 251)—trace one of the birds above. Stencil a row of birds on each side of the box, following Steps 3–5 on page 251).

3 Draw a zigzag pattern in pencil on the top and bottom borders. Paint over the pencil line in a contrasting colour.

4 Dip the eraser tip of the pencil in paint and print dots on the birds and along the zigzag borders.

GARDEN

11

CRESS EGGHEADS

you will need...

Clean egg shells, tops taken off

Fabric, wool + coloured paper scraps

Cardboard tube, from toilet roll

Lolly sticks, one for each egg

Cotton wool

Cress seeds

Sequins, stickers, buttons

Paints

Paintbrushes

Felt tip pens

Scissors

Glue

Wait for leaves to appear before you snip the cress for a sandwich!

Stick on round stickers for eyes, and a pair of gold reinforcement rings for earrings.

Make a moustache and eyebrows from short fringes of wool, and glue on a fabric tie over a paper shirt.

This cress pup has balloon ears and a wool tail.

COOL STUFF

12

making the cress eggheads...

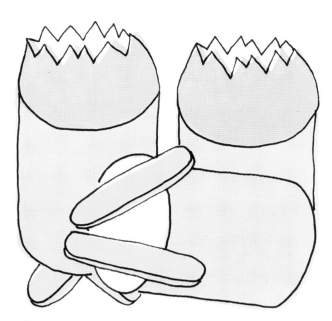

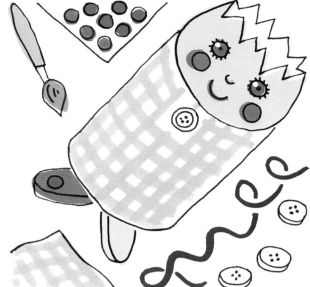

1 Cut a lolly stick in half and glue the 2 pieces to the bottom of a tube. Balance an egg shell on the top of the tube.

2 Paint or draw a face on the egg. Use stickers, buttons and fabric to decorate the tube body. Paint the feet.

3 Carefully fill the egg shell with cotton wool. Sprinkle with water and then with cress seeds. Put the egghead in a dark place.

4 When the green shoots appear, move the egghead to a bright place. Sprinkle water on the cotton wool every day.

GARDEN

13

MINIATURE GARDEN

you will need...

Wooden fruit crate

Lolly sticks, cut
　in half

2 beads, 2 buttons

Paints + paintbrushes

Felt tip pens

Dried split peas or
　lentils, or both

Silver foil

Assorted coloured
　paper

Wooden skewer,
　cut in half

Fabric, wool + string
　scraps

Matchbox drawer

Matchsticks

Cotton reel, cork

Paper clip

Cocktail paper
　umbrella

Scissors

Glue

Glue paper flowers to the walls of the crate, and glue green fabric to a corner post to make a tree.

Add details – to the flowers, cat, grass, table and wheelbarrow – with felt tip pen.

Glue a combination of dried split peas and lentils to the path to create different textures.

Glue the butterflies to the fence or the walls of the crate.

making a miniature garden...

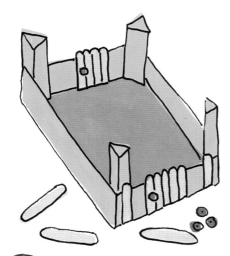

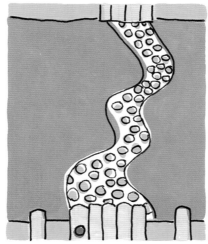

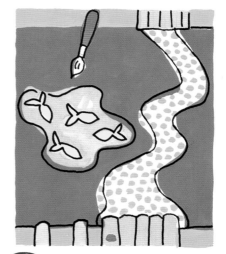

1 Glue lolly sticks – rounded end up – around the crate to make a fence and gates. Glue bead handles on the gates.

2 On the base of the crate, draw a path and paint glue on it. Pour split peas onto the path to cover it. Shake off the extra split peas.

3 Paint the rest of the base green for grass. Glue on a pond cut from foil, and glue on yellow paper fish to swim in it.

4 Glue a bead to one end of each piece of skewer. Glue the skewers to opposite corners of the crate. Glue tiny fabric clothes (copy the ones on page 14) to wool. Tie the wool to the skewers.

5 For the wheelbarrow, glue button wheels on a matchbox and add matchstick handles. For the table, glue a fabric tablecloth onto the reel, and push the umbrella through a tiny hole in the middle.

6 The cat is a painted cork with glued-on matchstick legs, paper ears and a wool tail. For the butterfly, fix a paper clip body to wings cut from blue paper (copy the ones above).

15

TOPIARY SHAPES

you will need...

For the Dinosaur Topiary

Wire or heavy duty garden
   wire, about 1 m (1 yd)
Fine wire scraps
Fuse wire, or other
   strong extra-fine wire
Plant pot
Paper
Pencil
Pliers
A few pieces of broken
   clay pot
Potting compost
2 small climbing
   plants
Plant ties
Assorted beads
Scissors

As the climbers grow, train them to the dinosaur shape using plant ties.

A wire flower with a zigzag stem makes a good topiary shape.

This simple topiary shape is the perfect way to display a flowering climber.

Heavy duty garden wire is strong, yet easy to shape without pliers – and it won't rust.

16

making a topiary shape...

Dinosaur

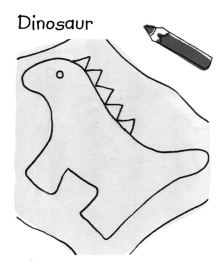

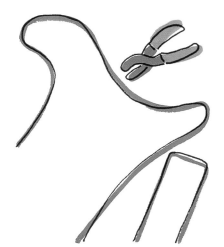

1 Draw the rough shape of a dinosaur on paper. It should be about 40 cm (16 in) long, and about 30 cm (12 in) high.

2 Bend one piece of wire to the dinosaur shape, using the pliers. Leave about 25 cm (10 in) extra wire at each end. Bend another piece of wire for the inside of the legs.

3 Bend wire in a zigzag and attach it with fuse wire to the back of the dinosaur. Hang a coil of fine wire from the top of the head with fuse wire, to form an eye.

4 Put the dinosaur wire in the pot. Push the extra wire through the holes in the base, bend to lie flat under the pot and cut off the excess. Repeat for the inner leg wire.

5 Put pieces of broken clay in the pot, and fill with compost. Plant the climbers, one at each leg. Fix the climbing shoots to the wire with plant ties.

6 Loop fine wire round the pot and twist the ends together. Thread beads onto spirals made by coiling the wire round a pencil. Hook 2 or more spirals on the wire.

SCARECROW
you will need...

Garden canes, one long 2 m (2 yd) +
3 shorter 1 m (1 yd)

Twine

Pair of old rubber gloves

Large plastic plant pot

Old pair of trousers, a shirt with
 buttons + a stretchy jumper

2 buttons

Acrylic paints

Paintbrushes

Coloured plastic
 shopping bags,
 cut into strips

Sewing thread

Needle

Straw

Scissors

Waterproof glue

Use old clothes in a large
child or adult size if you can - they
will pull on more easily over the
frame and the gloves.

Don't stuff the
scarecrow too full - just
enough to fill out the
clothes and gloves
a little.

Push the cane into
the soil of the vegetable
patch, and listen to the wind
fluttering in the flags and the
scarecrow's hair!

making a scarecrow...

1 Bind a short cane across the long (body) cane for arms, using twine. Bind two canes on lower down, for legs. Stuff the gloves with straw and tie with twine to the arms. Upend the pot on the neck, for a head. Push cane through draining hole.

2 Pull on the shirt and trousers, making the long cane go through a hole cut between the trouser legs. Tie the ankles with twine. Stuff the shirt body and trousers with straw. Tie the waist with twine. Remove the pot. Pull on the jumper. Tie the wrists with twine.

3 Upend the pot and glue on button eyes. Paint a nose, mouth and cheeks with acrylic paint. Glue on strips of plastic for hair, and a zigzag strip of plastic for a beard.

4 Replace the pot on the cane. Cut lots of small flags and streamers from plastic strips. Glue or sew them on all over the arms, legs and body of the scarecrow.

FLOWER WHEELS

you will need...

For the Strawberry Wheel

A level patch of soil, clear of
  weeds + stones

Garden cane (no sharp points)

Small stick

Twine, about 50 cm (20 in)

Sunflower seedling, or seed

Lettuce seeds

Chives seeds

Straw, a small bag

10-12 strawberry plant seedlings

For the lobelia wheel, use a mixture of purple lobelia and bright yellow/orange marigolds for the outer ring and pink lobelia for central initial 'F'.

Alpine strawberries are tiny and sweet, but any small variety will do.

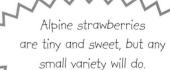

The straw stops the strawberries getting too wet.

making a flower wheel...

Strawberry wheel

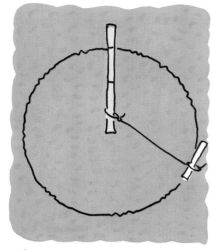

1 Push the cane into the soil in the centre of the patch. Tie twine to it and to a small stick, about 25 cm (10 in) away. Mark a circle in the soil, keeping the twine taut.

2 In the same way, but with the stick tied only 15 cm (6 in) from the centre, draw a smaller circle inside the first circle. Divide the inner circle into 4 with the stick.

3 Plant a sunflower seed or seedling in the centre of the wheel, next to the cane. You will need to tie the sunflower to the cane as it grows taller.

4 Scatter lettuce seeds in 2 opposite quarters of the wheel, and chives seeds in the remaining quarters. Cover with a thin layer of soil and gently water the bed.

5 Plant the strawberry seedlings in the soil of the outer ring. (They should be evenly spaced.) Gently spread straw around and between the strawberry plants.

6 Keep the flower wheel moist and free of weeds. Snip off chives as you need them, and scatter more seeds to replace the lettuces you have picked.

GARDEN

21

SUNFLOWER STICKS

Use different colours and thicknesses of twine and string for different textures.

Glue or tie one or 2 leaves and perhaps a snail to each sunflower stem, or tie/glue a colourful snail to its own cane!

Paint natural string or twine with acrylic paint to achieve the colours you want.

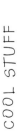

you will need...

Polystyrene, or
    frozen pizza backing
Assorted twine + string
Acrylic paints
Paintbrushes
Varnish
Insulation tape

Double-sided tape
Garden canes
    (no sharp points)
Assorted beads
Plant ties
Scissors
Waterproof glue

Use these bright flowers and snails in winter when the garden is looking a bit dull. Alternatively, they can be used as plant supports.

making a sunflower stick...

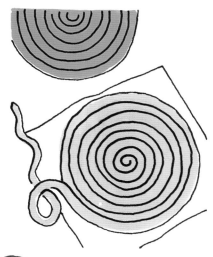

1 Stick double-sided tape on a 6 cm (2³⁄₈ in) square of polystyrene. Make a coil of twine or string on the sticky square. Cut the polystyrene around the coil.

2 For the sunflower, cut 2 flower shapes from polystyrene. Paint them red or yellow. Glue a string coil to the centre of each flower. Varnish the flower all over.

3 Tape or glue a cane to the back of one flower. Glue the other flower to the cane. (Don't try to stick the flowers together, and make sure the coils face outwards.)

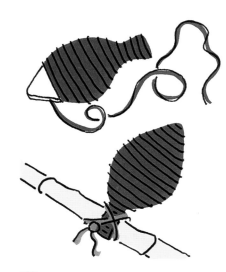

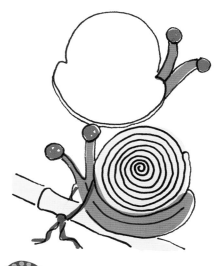

4 Stick double-sided tape to a leaf cut from polystyrene (trace one above). Wind green twine round it, covering both sides. Varnish. Glue or tie to the cane.

5 For the snail, stick a folded string body and a coiled string shell to a polystyrene base (trace this one). Varnish. Glue beads to the antennae. Tie to the cane.

6 Tie a leggy plant to a sunflower stick for support, or simply pot your flower stick and enjoy year-round colour. Fix the snail to a cane or glue on a pot as decoration.

OUTDOOR
wind wizardry

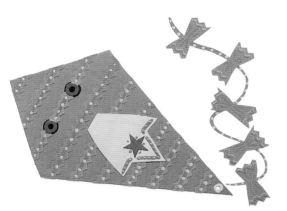

Pinwheels

Miniature Kites

Papier Mâché Mobiles

Wind Chimes

Aeroplanes

Dragon Birdscarer

Crocodile Whirligig

25

PINWHEELS
you will need...

For the Yellow Spotted Pinwheel

Yellow paper, about 10-18 cm
   (4-7 in) square

Green paper, a scrap

Ruler

Felt tip pens

Stickers

Pin

Small bead

Plastic drinking straw

Piece of cork

Scissors

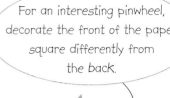

For an interesting pinwheel, decorate the front of the paper square differently from the back.

This pinwheel has a flower centre, flowers on each of the curled corners, and a spotty design on the front.

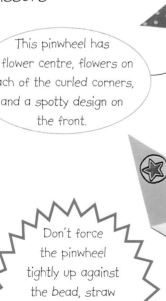

Don't force the pinwheel tightly up against the bead, straw and cork - keep it slightly loose so that it spins more easily.

making a pinwheel...

Yellow Spot

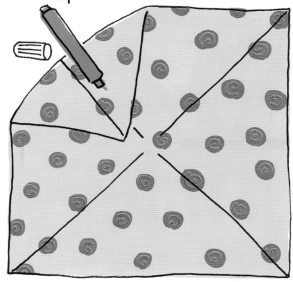

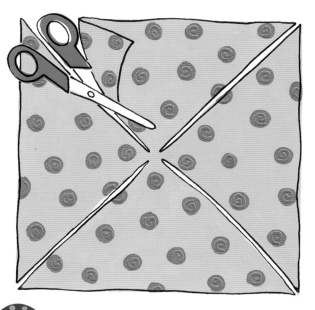

1 Decorate both sides of the paper with felt tip pens and stickers. With a ruler, draw 2 diagonal lines joining the opposite corners of the square.

2 Cut along the lines, but stop about 1 cm (¼ in) from the centre. You now have 4 triangles, joined in the centre. Fold every alternate point into the centre.

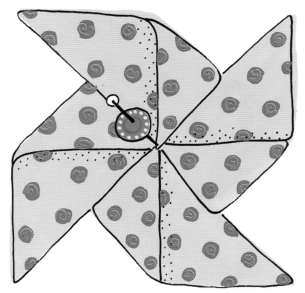

3 Cut a small circle, about 1.5 cm (½ in) in diameter, from green paper. Push a pin through the middle of the circle, then through alternate corners of the 4 triangles.

4 At the back, push the pin through first the bead, then the end of the straw. Bury the point in the cork, but keep the pinwheel, bead and straw slightly loose on the pin.

MINIATURE KITES

you will need...

Thick coloured paper, about 30 cm (12 in) square

Coloured paper, a large sheet

Paints

Paintbrushes

Stickers

Cord or thick thread, about 10 m (10 yd)

3 square stickers, or pieces of sticky tape

Hole punch

Scissors

Glue

These kites are designed to be used in a light breeze - they will tear if you fly them in a gale-force wind!

Decorate your Flying Fish with bright spots or squiggles of paint, and don't forget a big, watchful eye.

Twist paper or crepe paper rectangles at intervals down the tail, and add a dot of glue to hold each one in place.

The square stickers prevent the cord from tearing the paper.

making a miniature kite...

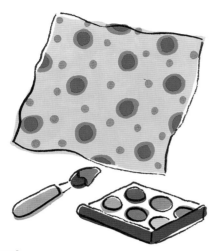

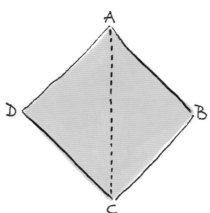

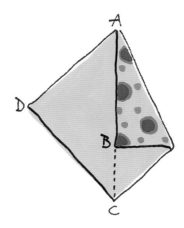

1 Decorate the square of thick paper with paint or felt pen on both sides.

2 Fold the square in half along one diagonal (AC). Open the square out again.

3 Copy the picture above to fold the side AB to meet the centre fold. Fold AD to meet the centre fold in the same way. Flatten the folds.

4 Stick a square sticker on the tip of the kite, punch a hole and tie 1 m (1 yd) of cord through it. Twist 3 x 6 cm (1¼ x 2½ in) paper rectangles onto the tail.

5 Stick square stickers on the corners folded in at the back. Punch a hole in each. Loop cord through the holes and knot it, leaving the rest of the cord dangling.

6 Turn the kite over. On the front, paint a large eye and a fin in a contrasting colour. Fly the flying fish kite by the long piece of cord tied at the back.

WIND WIZARDRY

PAPIER MÂCHÉ MOBILES

you will need...

For the Birds Mobile

Corrugated cardboard,
about 20 x 25 cm (8 x 10 in)

Craft knife (*be careful!*)

Newspaper, cut into strips

Paints

Paintbrushes

Felt tip pens

Stickers

Patterned wrapping paper

Paper, cut into tall
triangles (isosceles)

Varnish

Thin knitting needle

Cord, about 75 cm (30 in)

Darning needle

Glue, diluted with water

Glue

You can make the mobile as long as you like – just make enough birds and beads to fit your cord.

The sun, moon and stars are made from papier mâché covered in shiny foil and decorated with sequins or drawn patterns.

Draw patterns on the on the foil with a dry ballpoint pen to create this embossed look.

Paint the birds on both sides, or glue on patterned wrapping paper for added decoration.

making a papier mâché mobile...

Birds mobile

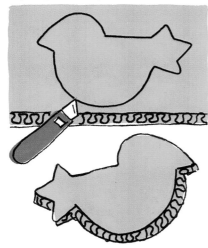

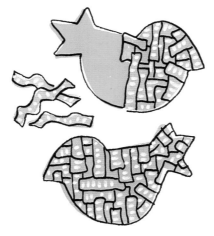

1 Cut 5 or 6 bird shapes from corrugated card (trace the ones on page 30) with a craft knife. An adult should help you. The ridges should run from top to bottom.

2 Paste a layer of newspaper strips onto the birds, using dilute glue and a paintbrush (see page 245). Cover both sides and the cut edges. Allow to dry.

3 Paint the birds, or glue patterned paper on both sides. Decorate with stickers or glued-on paper and add beak, eye and wing details with felt pen. Varnish.

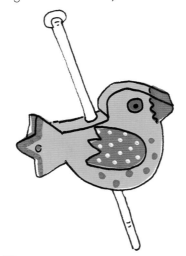

4 Make beads by rolling the paper triangles around the knitting needle. Glue the point of each triangle. When dry, slide off the needle. Paint and varnish the beads.

5 Gently push the knitting needle through the middle of each bird, from top to bottom - find the gap between 2 ridges in the corrugated cardboard.

6 Tie a loop in the end of the cord. Then use the darning needle to thread birds and beads alternately on the cord. Make a knot below each bird/bead to stop it slipping.

WIND WIZARDRY

31

WIND CHIMES

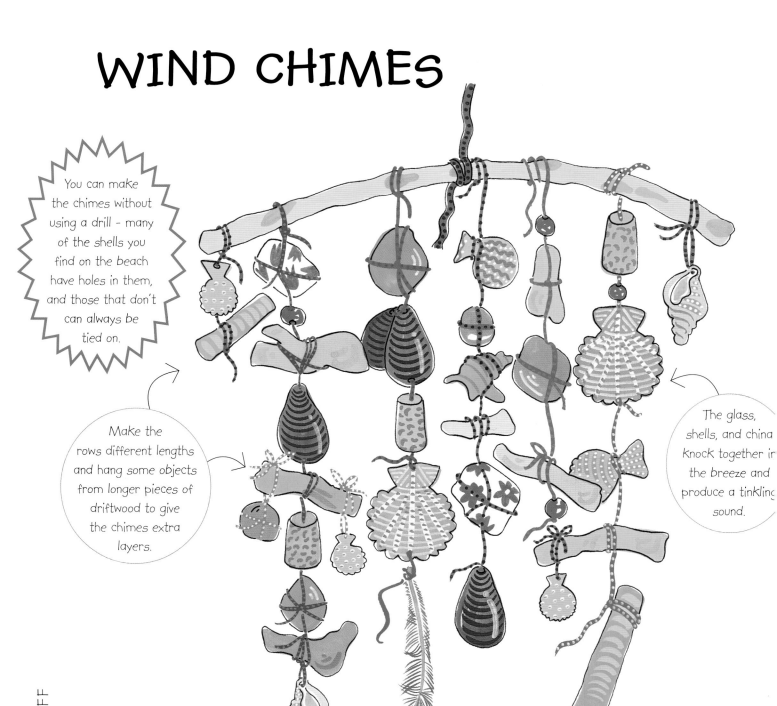

You can make the chimes without using a drill - many of the shells you find on the beach have holes in them, and those that don't can always be tied on.

Make the rows different lengths and hang some objects from longer pieces of driftwood to give the chimes extra layers.

The glass, shells, and china knock together in the breeze and produce a tinkling sound.

you will need...

Shells, feathers, cork + bits of driftwood

Driftwood, one long piece, or garden cane

Fragments of weathered china and glass (no sharp pieces)

Twine, rope + string

Darning needle

making the wind chimes...

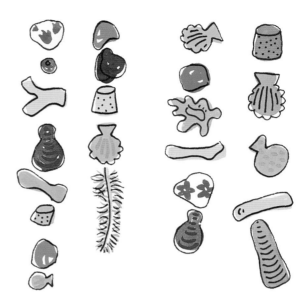

1 Tie a 50 cm (20 in) length of rope or string to the middle of the long piece of driftwood. Make a loop at the other end to hang the chimes from.

2 Arrange the shells, cork, wood, glass and china into rows of different lengths. Put light things like feathers and tiny shells at the bottom. Cut the cork and wood into small pieces.

3 Ask an adult to drill holes in the shells and wood. Make holes in the cork with a needle. Thread objects onto the twine using a darning needle, or simply loop and tie the twine round each one.

4 Tie the rows of objects loosely to the big piece of driftwood. Try to balance the weight evenly. Hang the chimes and adjust the dangling rows left and right until the wood hangs level and the objects knock against each other.

WIND WIZARDRY

33

AEROPLANES

you will need...

- Polystyrene, or frozen pizza backing
- Craft knife (be careful!)
- Paints
- Paintbrushes
- Felt tip pens
- Stickers
- Sticky putty

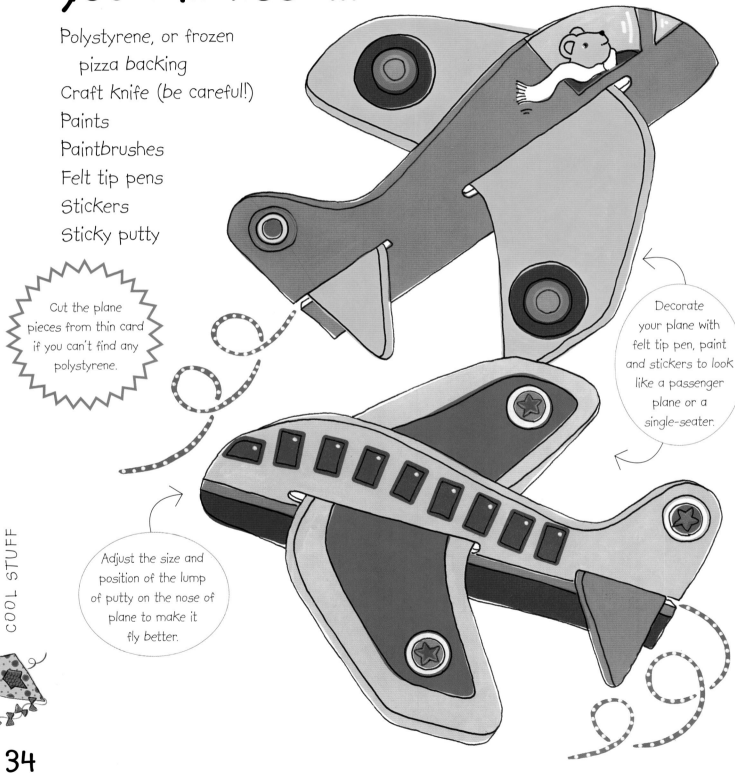

Cut the plane pieces from thin card if you can't find any polystyrene.

Decorate your plane with felt tip pen, paint and stickers to look like a passenger plane or a single-seater.

Adjust the size and position of the lump of putty on the nose of plane to make it fly better.

making an aeroplane...

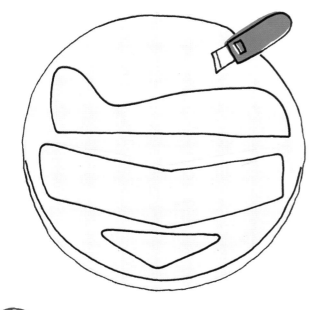

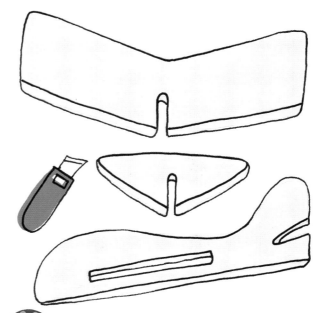

1 Cut the 3 pieces of the plane from polystyrene, using the template on page 253. (An adult should help you.)

2 Cut a notch in the *body*, *wing* and *tail* sections and a *slit* in the body of the plane. Use the picture above as a guide.

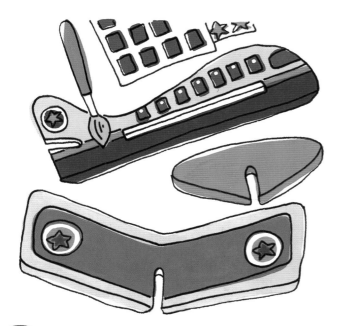

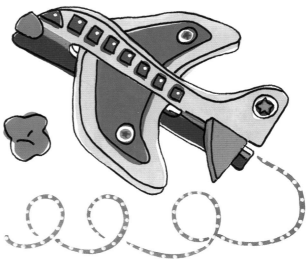

3 Paint one side of each piece. Allow to dry before painting the other side. Decorate with stickers for windows, and wing and tail markings.

4 Push the *wing* section through the slit in the body and slot in place. Slot the tail in place at the back of the body. Press a small lump of putty on the nose.

DRAGON BIRDSCARER

you will need...

5 garden canes (no sharp points)

Raffia in several bright colours

2 orange plastic bags, fronts + backs
   separated

Large sheet of
   flexible plastic
   (available from
   DIY stores and
   large garden
   centres)

Waterproof felt
   tip pens or
   acrylic paint

Insulation tape

Scissors

Glue

Push the canes into the soil where
birds (or cats) are a problem – and let
the wind do the rest!

Use extra
canes and plastic
bags of any colour
to make a longer
tail.

Make the
Dragon's face as
garish – and fierce
– as you can.

36

making a dragon birdscarer...

1 Draw a dragon's face on the plastic sheet. Cut out. Paint the face with acrylic paint or waterproof felt pens.

2 Cut a slit for a mouth. Cut a tongue from the carton and paint it red. Poke it through the slit and tape it in place at the back.

3 Glue multicoloured bunches of raffia to the back of the dragon's face for the hair, and over the slit for the tongue for a beard.

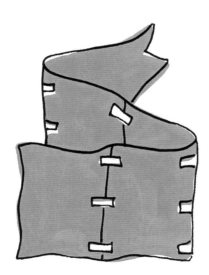

4 Tape a cane to each side of the face, at the back. Hide the top of each cane behind the raffia hair.

5 Tape the plastic sheets together to make a long tail. Cut a V-shaped notch in the last sheet.

6 Tape a cane at the join between each pair of plastic sheets. Cut lots of pennants from plastic bags. Tape pennants to the tops of the canes and the tail.

WIND WIZARDRY

37

CROCODILE WHIRLIGIG

you will need...

3 plastic milk containers
Thin garden cane
6 beads, big
     enough to
     thread onto
     the cane
Green + blue acrylic
     paints
Paintbrushes
Waterproof felt tip pens
Varnish
Insulation tape
Plastic drinking
     straw, cut
     into 3 cm
     (1¼ in) lengths
Craft knife (be careful!)
Scissors
Glue

If your beads
are too big or too
small, wrap insulation
tape around the cane
above and below each
crocodile instead.

Fold back on
a vertical side of
each triangle for
the best wind-
catching fins.

Paint each crocodile a
different colour, and pick
out the details in a
contrasting colour.

38

making a crocodile whirligig...

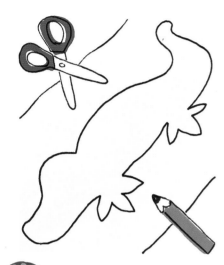

1 Draw a crocodile shape on the plastic container. Cut out 3 the same.

2 Mark 4 triangles on each crocodile, 2 at the front and 2 at the back. Cut 2 sides of each with the knife (an adult should help you). Fold back on the 3rd side.

3 Paint both sides of the crocodiles. On one side only, paint fins, a mouth, toes and eyes in a contrasting colour. Varnish.

4 Tape a piece of straw to the back of each crocodile, in the middle.

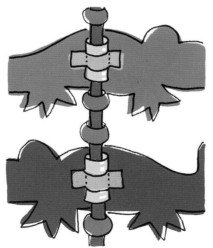

5 Thread the crocodiles onto the cane with a bead above and below each one. A dot of glue below each bead will stop it slipping.

6 Push the cane into the ground. The wind will catch the fins and spin the crocodiles on the cane.

OUTDOOR
waterplay

Cork Rafts +
Ducks

'Gone Fishing'
Game

Water Xylophone

Miniature
Harbour

CORK RAFTS + DUCKS

you will need...

For the Rafts

4 corks

Coloured paper, small sheets

Stickers

2 plastic drinking straws

Craft knife (*be careful!*)

Scissors

Waterproof glue

Decorate the sails in bold colours, and add paper flags.

The masts can be glued to any of the corks.

These ducks have painted paper bodies threaded onto cocktail sticks for support.

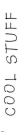

making a cork raft...

1 Glue the corks side by side to form the raft. Press them together firmly until the glue is completely dry.

2 Cut 2 square sails from paper about the length of a cork, and decorate them with stickers. Cut 2 flags from paper and add stickers for decoration.

3 Cut a slit at the top and bottom of each sail, in the centre. Thread a straw through each slit. Glue a flag to the top of each straw mast.

4 Cut a small slit in the middle of 2 corks. Cut the straws to the right length. Flatten the cut ends and push each into a slit. Glue the straw masts in place.

WATERPLAY

43

'GONE FISHING' GAME

you will need...

Plastic milk containers, or other white
   plastic containers
Acrylic paints
Paintbrushes
Waterproof felt tip pens
5 corks
Craft Knife (*be careful!*)
Fine wire scraps
Sticky putty
Garden cane (no sharp points)
String, about 1 m (1 yd)
Bowl, filled with water
Scissors

Use enough
putty to keep the creatures
vertical in the water.

The corks
will Keep the
creatures from
sinking and
escaping your
hook!

Paint the
creatures in
bright colours which
will show up even
when they are
under water.

Make the loops at
least 1.5 cm (1/2 in) in
diameter, otherwise you
will find it very difficult
to catch anything!

making the fishing game...

1 Draw a crab, starfish, octopus and 2 fish on the white plastic. Cut them out with scissors.

2 Decorate the sea creatures on both sides with acrylic paint or waterproof felt pens. Make them as bright and colourful as you can.

3 Cut a slit along the length of each cork with a craft knife. (An adult should help you with this.) Slide a creature onto each cork.

4 Make a loop from a scrap of wire. Twist the ends together. Push the sharp ends into the top of a cork. Repeat for all the creatures.

5 Press one or 2 small lumps of putty onto the bottom of each creature to make sure it hangs vertically in the water.

6 Make a hook from a scrap of wire, tie it to the string and tie the end of the string to the cane. Float the creatures in water.

WATERPLAY

45

WATER XYLOPHONE

you will need...

6 glass bottles of similar size
Assorted shells + beads
Raffia + string scraps
Fine wire scraps
Blue + green ink or
 food colouring
Metal spoon
Jug
Scissors
Glue

Blue and green bottles need only be filled with plain water.

Tap the bottles gently with the spoon to hear their different notes.

Use a different colour - or depth of colour - in each bottle, for an attractive effect.

making a water xylophone...

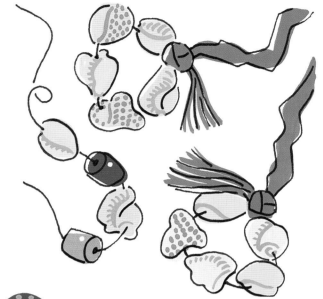

① Glue beads or shells onto the bottles, or thread beads and shells on string or raffia and hang round the necks of the bottles.

② For shell tassels, thread shells on wire, twist the wire round the ends of the raffia and tie the raffia round the bottle neck.

③ Add ink or food colouring to a jug of water. Use more or less ink/food colouring to get different depths of colour.

④ Line up the bottles. Pour a little water in the first bottle, more in the next, and so on. The last bottle should be nearly full.

WATERPLAY

47

MINIATURE HARBOUR

you will need...

Large *blue* or *green* plastic bowl
Acrylic paints + paintbrushes
Waterproof felt tip pens
Plastic bottle
2 plastic margarine tubs, with lids
Fromage frais or small yoghurt pot
Polystyrene, or frozen pizza backing
Thin card, a small
    sheet
Orange +
    grey paper,
    a small sheet
Silver foil, a scrap
Black embroidery thread
Small pebbles or sand
2 red lids
2 corks
Matchsticks
Stickers
Red bead
Old white felt
    tip pen lids
Craft knife
Scissors
Glue

The paper details on the penguins and lighthouse will be spoiled if you get them wet - take care!

You may find it easier to glue the matchsticks ar thread into a kind ladder, and then gl the completed railing to the lighthouse.

You can use any plastic food container for the base of the lighthouse and the ship; take-away cartons are a good choice.

Don't fill the bowl with wate put in just eno to let your who and ship floo freely.

When you have made the lighthouse, boat and whales, position them in a large bowl and partially fill with water.

making a miniature harbour...

1 Paint red and white stripes on the bottle and a black strip around the top. Use stickers for a door and windows. Don't paint or decorate the bottom 6 cm (2³⁄₈ in) of the bottle.

2 Paint the small pot yellow. Add hatching with felt pen. Upend and glue to the top of the bottle. Glue a bead on the top. Glue matchsticks round the black stripe, and glue on a black thread rail.

3 Draw round the bottle base on one tub lid. Cut out the circle. Paint the tub and lid brown. Put pebbles in the base, replace the lid and push the bottle through it. Put the lighthouse in the bowl.

4 Cut holes for the 2 funnels in the tub lid. Paint the tub and lid white and add port holes on both sides. Glue polystyrene smoke (copy the smoke above) to the lids. Push the lids through the holes.

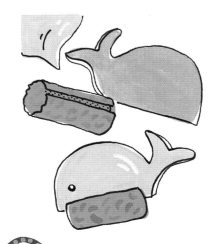

5 Cut 2 whales from card. Cover with foil. Cut a slit along the length of each cork with the craft knife (an adult should help you). Slide a whale onto each cork.

6 Paint old pen lids black, leaving an oval white. Paint on eyes and a beak. Cut feet from orange paper and wings from grey paper (copy the ones above) and glue to the penguins.

49

OUTDOOR
games to play

Penguin Skittles

Throw the Dog
a Bone

Knock the Parrots
off their Perch

Cup-and-Ball
Game

Skipping Rope

PENGUIN SKITTLES

you will need...

10 plastic bottles and lids, all the
    same size
Plastic bag or old rubber gloves
Acrylic paints
Paintbrushes
Felt tip pens
Jug
Sand (optional)
Small ball

The sand or water helps keep the bottles steady until you are ready to bowl them over!

Add a felt pen pupil to each eye and make the penguins look in different directions, just for fun.

Paint the lids for added colour if you like.

making the penguin skittles...

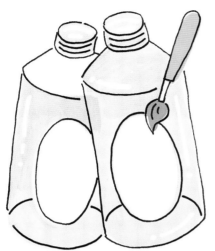

1 Paint a white oval tummy on each bottle. Paint the neck of each bottle white. Allow to dry.

2 Paint the rest of each bottle black. Take care not to spoil the white areas. Allow to dry.

3 Paint (or draw in felt pen) a red bow tie, an orange beak, blue/green eyes and black pupils.

4 Cut up the plastic bag to make 2 feet for each penguin. Glue them to the base of the bottle. Draw on wings with felt pen.

5 Quarter fill each bottle with sand (or water), using a jug. Try not to wet the paint. Replace the lids and tighten.

6 Set the skittles up in a group. Bowl the ball towards them and see how many penguins you can knock over in one go!

THROW THE DOG A BONE

Make sure your beanbags will fit through the mouth you have cut.

Prop the cardboard against a wall, or against a pair of small plant pots.

You could throw the dog a tennis ball instead of the beanbags.

Make small square beanbags as a simpler alternative.

you will need...

Thick cardboard, about 24 cm (9½ in) square

Pencil

Craft Knife (be careful!)

Paints + paintbrushes

Dried beans

Hessian or fabric, about 16 cm (6½ in) square

Sewing thread

Needle

Scissors + pinking shears

Glue

making a dog and bones...

1 On the cardboard, draw a border and a dog with a mouth about 7.5 cm (3 in) in diameter. Cut out the mouth with a craft knife (an adult should help you).

2 Paint the dog, the background and the border in bright contrasting colours. Copy the picture above or choose your own colour combinations.

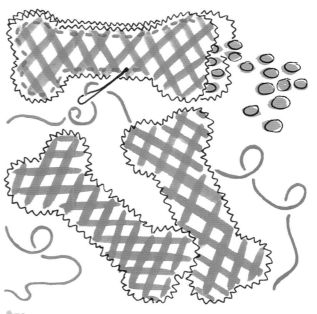

3 Cut out 2 ears from hessian. Glue the top third of each ear to the cardboard, leaving the bottom two-thirds to flap free.

4 For a beanbag, cut 2 bone shapes from fabric using pinking shears. Sew them together, leaving a gap. Stuff with beans and sew up the gap.

GAMES TO PLAY

KNOCK THE PARROTS OFF THEIR PERCH

you will need...

6 fizzy drink cans, clean + empty
Dried beans
Sticky tape
Thin card, a small sheet
Acrylic paints
Paintbrushes
Felt tip pens
Stickers
2 plant pots
2 long garden
　canes
Tennis ball

Use bright acrylic paint and felt tip pens to make brilliant plumage for your parrots.

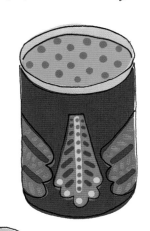

Paint or draw the eyes and add round stickers for the finishing touch.

Decorate the plant pots with acrylic paint – if you have permission!

Throw the ball and try to knock the parrots off their perch!

making the parrots + perch...

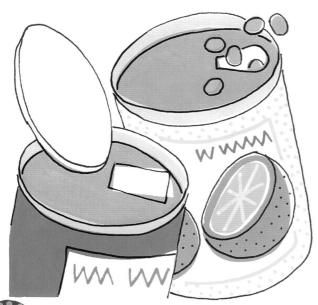

1 Cut 6 circles from card to fit the top of a can (draw round the end of a can). Pour a handful of beans into each can. Tape over the hole. Glue a circle to the top of each can.

2 Paint the cans all over in bright colours. Paint the card tops a contrasting colour. Allow to dry.

3 Paint (or draw) the parrots' eyes, beaks, wings and tails. Decorate the tops with spots and stripes.

4 Rest the canes about 5 cm (2 in) apart on the upended pots. Stand the parrots on their cane perch.

GAMES TO PLAY

57

CUP-AND-BALL GAME

you will need...

For one Cup-and-Ball

2 yoghurt pots, clean + empty

Paints

Paintbrushes

Felt tip pens

Foam shapes or scraps

Stickers

Masking tape

Ribbon or braid ('ric-rac') scraps

Coloured paper scraps

Ping pong ball

Darning or knitting needle

String or cord, about
50 cm (20 in)

Scissors

Glue

This Funny Face has pointy foam ears and a moustache made from a strip of plastic.

The knot hidden in the top pot keeps the string secure.

Throw the ball up and try to catch it in your Funny Face cup.

making a cup-and-ball game...

1 Paint the yoghurt pots. Paint a pattern on one, or use stickers. Glue a foam nose and sticker eyes to the other.

2 Glue the bases of the pots together. Tape over the join to strengthen it. Glue ribbon, braid or coloured paper over the join.

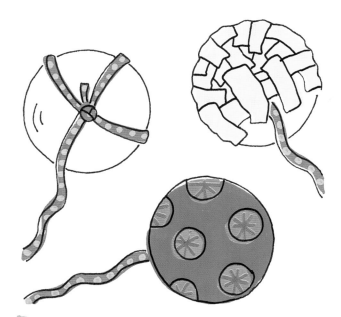

3 Knot the string onto the ball. Stick tape all over the ball. Cover the knot with tape, but leave the string dangling free. Paint the ball and add stickers for decoration.

4 Make a hole in the bases of the 2 pots with a darning needle. Push the string through the hole in the bottom pot. Knot the end to hold it in the top pot.

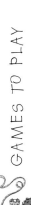

GAMES TO PLAY

59

SKIPPING ROPE

you will need...

Coloured nylon cord in 4 colours:
  3 colours each about 2 m (2 yd)
  A scrap of a fourth colour
Assorted wooden beads
Scissors

This yellow beaded cord has been tied on at both ends to decorate the finished skipping rope.

Remember that plaiting will shorten your rope, so start off with a generous length - you can always cut it!

Make a longer skipping rope if you plan to skip with your friends.

making a skipping rope...

1 Knot the 3 strands of rope together at one end, leaving about 25 cm (10 in) free below the knot.

2 Hook the knot onto a coat hook or cupboard handle to hold it still. Plait the rope, keeping the tension even as you go.

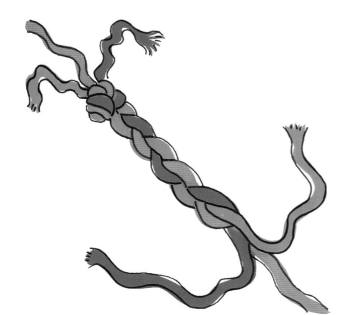

3 Stop plaiting about 25 cm (10 in) before the end. Knot the 3 strands of rope together.

4 Thread beads onto each strand of rope, tying knots to hold them in place. Tie a small, beaded cord just above the knots in the rope. Unravel the ends to make tassels.

GAMES TO PLAY

61

PARTY TIME
birthdays

Birthday Banner

Animal Balloons

Party Cups

Party Hats

Party Bags

Birthday T-shirts

BIRTHDAY BANNER

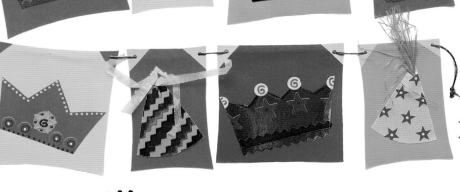

The triangles glued over the corners will stop the string from tearing the paper when the banner is hung up.

Use a gold marker pen, gold star stickers and gold paper to give extra sparkle to the banner.

Let your imagination run wild, and make each crown and party hat different.

You can make this party banner as long as your piece of string – just keep adding squares or rectangles!

you will need...

Assorted coloured paper, large sheets
Foil or gold paper, large sheets
Raffia or wool or tissue strips,
    cut into 15 cm (6 in) lengths
Wool or string or raffia, about 3 m (3 yd)

Stickers
Felt tip pens
Hole punch
Scissors
Glue

making a birthday banner...

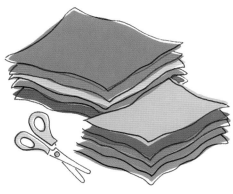

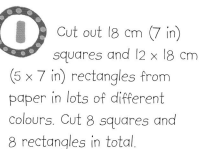

1 Cut out 18 cm (7 in) squares and 12 x 18 cm (5 x 7 in) rectangles from paper in lots of different colours. Cut 8 squares and 8 rectangles in total.

2 Cut 16 small 4 cm (1½ in) squares from coloured paper. Cut each in half, to make 2 triangles. Glue a triangle to the top 2 corners of the squares and rectangles. Punch holes in these corners.

3 Cut 8 crown and 8 cone shapes from foil and coloured paper. If you need any help, trace off the cone and crown shapes on page 70.

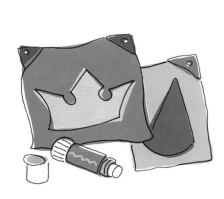

4 Glue a crown in the middle of each large square, and a cone in the middle of each rectangle. Make sure that the corners with triangles are at the top.

5 Glue small bunches of raffia, wool or tissue strips onto the cone hats. Decorate the crowns and hats with stickers, felt pens and glued-on paper shapes.

6 Thread a length of wool, string or raffia through the holes in the corners, alternating squares (crowns) and rectangles (cones) as you go.

65

ANIMAL BALLOONS

you will need...

For the Orange Cat Balloon

Orange balloon

Wool or narrow ribbon,
   about 75 cm (30 in)

Green or yellow
   round stickers

Foam scraps

Yellow plastic
   drinking straw

Orange fabric or
   paper scraps

Glue or double-sided tape

Felt tip pens

Scissors

Two white balloons covered with felt pen spots make delightful ears for this Dalmatian!

A bow round his neck makes this pooch look like a pedigree!

Miss Pig's ears and nose are cut from pieces of pink foam, and her eyes are blue stickers.

A long, green wiggly balloon makes a long, green wriggly caterpillar – just add sticker eyes and bright markings of your own design.

making an animal balloon...

Orange Cat

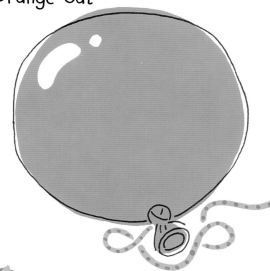

1 Blow up the balloon and Knot it. Tie a long piece of wool or ribbon to the Knot.

2 Stick on stickers for eyes and a circle of foam for a nose. Draw in the mouth and pupils of the eyes with felt pen.

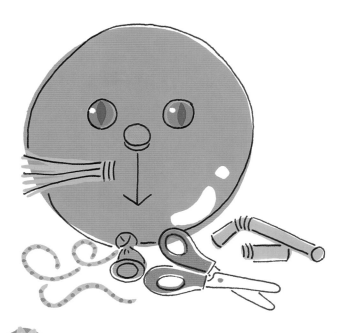

3 For the whiskers, cut the straw through the bend, and about 7.5 cm (3 in) below it. Cut this in half along its length. In each half make 6-8 cuts up to the bend. Glue the bend of the straw to the balloon.

4 Cut 2 ears out of fabric or paper (a bulgy triangle makes a good ear shape). Glue an oval of white foam to the front of each ear. Glue the ears in place on the balloon.

67

PARTY CUPS

you will need...

For the Frog Cup

Paper cup

Plastic drinking straw

Dark green, light green, orange +
   yellow paper, small sheets

Round yellow stickers

Paints

Paintbrush

Felt tip pens

Craft knife (*be careful!*)

Scissors, pinking shears

Glue

Snail's feelers are
made from small
beads threaded onto
paper string and
glued in place.

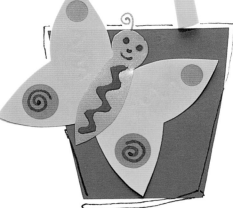

Draw around the two
ends of your cup to get
the flower circles you
need.

Bee's delicate
wings are cut from
pale blue tissue.

making a frog cup...

1 Cut a frog body/head/front legs from dark green paper and 2 back legs from light green paper.

2 Glue the frog's back legs to the back of the body. Stick on yellow stickers for eyes. Paint on the details, or use a felt pen. Glue the frog onto the cup.

3 From paper, cut a large flower shape. With pinking shears, cut a smaller paper circle and glue on the front of the flower.

4 Cut 2 slits in the centre of the flower with the craft knife (an adult should help you). Thread the straw through the slits.

BIRTHDAYS

PARTY HATS
you will need...

For the Cone Hat

Thin coloured card, about 40 cm
  (16 in) square
Assorted coloured paper, small sheets
Assorted coloured tissue paper,
  scraps cut into thin strips
Star stickers + round stickers
Shirring elastic, about 40 cm
  (16 in)
Darning needle
Pencil
Pinking shears
Scissors
Glue or double-sided
  tape or stapler

Make tiny tassels
by folding a bunch of
4 tissue strips in half,
and holding the fold
down with a bright
sticker.

Staple the elastic to the
inside of the hat on each
side if you prefer.

Cut a zigzag down
one long edge of a strip
of gold card to make
this glittering crown.

Big shiny
stickers look like
crown jewels, and a
scattering of tiny stars
- one on each point -
catch the light
and add extra
sparkle.

making a party hat...

Cone

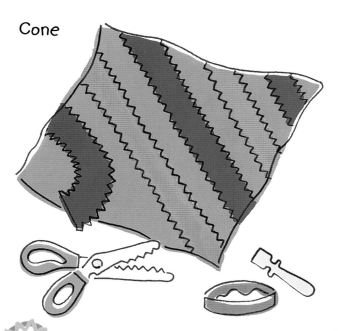

1 Cut strips of coloured paper using pinking shears. Glue the strips diagonally across the square of coloured card.

2 Draw around a dinner plate on the card. Cut out the circle with scissors. Cut away a quarter section (see page 246).

3 Decorate the card with stickers. Make small bunches of tissue strips into tiny tassels (see page 249), and stick them down with stickers. Make sure all the tassels hang away from the centre.

4 Glue, tape or staple the card into a cone to fit round your head. Stick a large tassel to the top. Make a hole on each side of the hat with the needle. Thread elastic through the holes and knot on the outside.

BIRTHDAYS

71

PARTY BAGS

you will need...

For the Flop-eared Bunny Bag

Blue paper, about 15 x 40 cm (6 x 16 in)

Pale pink crepe paper, about 10 cm
(4 in) square

Deep pink crepe paper, 2 strips each
about 1.5 x 8 cm (½ x 3¼ in)

2 pink balloons

Raffia, 2 lengths each
about 40 cm (16 in)

6 round blue stickers

Felt tip pens

Foam scrap

Hole punch

Pinking shears

Scissors

Glue

This dog is the proud owner of a brown crepe paper patch - and a sloppy balloon tongue!

A strip of foam makes a soft handle.

Make bags to suit a birthday theme, or try this simple flower, perfect for any party.

Paint the foam scrap if necessary before you glue it in place.

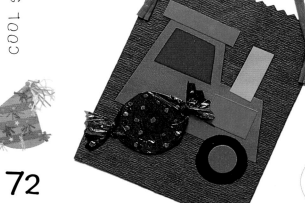

The tractor is cut from coloured paper and given a shiny sweet wrapper as a rear tyre.

making a party bag...

Flop-eared Bunny

1 Fold the blue paper in half. Trim the short ends with pinking shears. Glue on an oval cut from pale pink crepe paper. Glue on balloon ears.

2 Add stickers for eyes, and glue on the foam nose. Draw in a mouth with felt pen.

3 Cut the pieces of deep pink paper into very thin strips, stopping about 1.5 cm (½ in) from the end. Glue these whiskers on either side of the mouth.

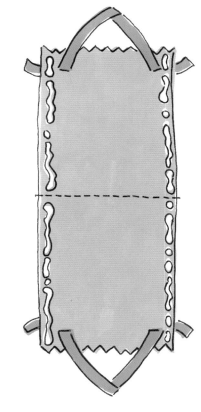

4 On the inside of the bag, put a sticker where you will make the holes for the 2 handles. Punch the holes (4 in all). Thread raffia or foam handles through the holes and knot on the outside.

5 Open out the bag and lay it wrong side up. Spread glue down each of the long sides.

6 Fold the bag in half again, pressing the 2 sides together and allow the glue to set. Staple the sides for extra strength.

BIRTHDAY T-SHIRTS

you will need...

For the No. 5 T-shirt

Cotton T-shirt

Yellow fabric, about 25 cm (10 in) square

Patterned fabric, about 25 cm (10 in) square

Fusible web (see page 248)

4 buttons

Paper

Sewing thread

Needle + pins

Iron (be careful!)

Make a birthday T-shirt to wear at your own party, or give it as a gift to a friend.

Choose fabric of your favourite colour, making sure that the number fabric shows up against the background fabric.

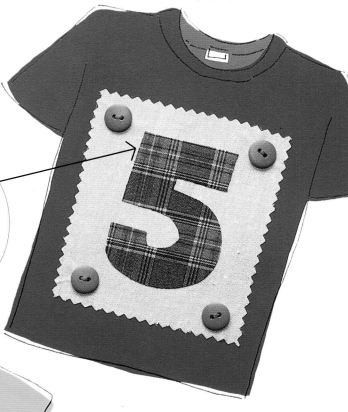

Cut out a petal pattern from bright background material and fuse on a circle of checked fabric for this sunflower T-shirt.

COOL STUFF

making a birthday T-shirt...

No. 5

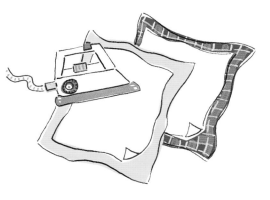

1 Iron fusible web to the wrong side of the yellow fabric and the patterned fabric (see page 248). An adult should help you with this.

2 Cut the yellow fabric to fit the T-shirt. Trim the edges of the yellow fabric with pinking shears.

3 Make a paper pattern of the number you need to fit on the yellow background fabric. Pin it to the right side of the patterned fabric and cut out.

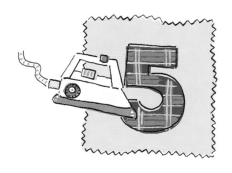

4 Remove the paper backing from the fabric number. Carefully place the number in the centre of the yellow fabric. Iron over the number to make it stick (an adult should help you).

5 Remove the paper backing from the yellow fabric. Place the yellow fabric on the front of the T-shirt. Iron over it to make it stick to the T-shirt (an adult should help you).

6 Sew a button to each corner of the yellow square, stitching through all the layers. Glue the buttons on if you prefer.

BIRTHDAYS

75

PARTY TIME
Easter holiday

Easter Paper Chain

'Rattle and Roll' Puzzle

Salt Dough Easter Tree

Royal Eggs

Decorated Eggs

Easter Bonnets

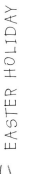

EASTER PAPER CHAIN

you will need...

For the Ducklings Paper Chain

White paper, strip of
    10 x 54 cm (4 x 21½ in)
Pencil + felt tip pen
Paints + paintbrushes
Scissors

Use a longer strip of paper - or tape 2 strips together - for a longer paper chain.

Carefully cut away the paper under the beak.

The Bunnies touch noses and tails at the paper folds and edges.

making a paper chain...

Ducklings

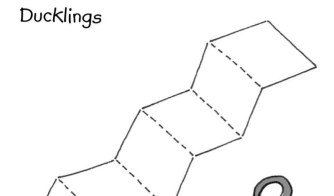

1 Fold the paper strip concertina-style 5 times. You should have a *book* about 9 cm x 10 cm (3½ x 4 in).

2 Draw a duckling in pencil on the top page of the *book*. Make sure the tummy, *beak* and tail reach the edge or fold at the sides. Cut round the top of the duckling through all the layers.

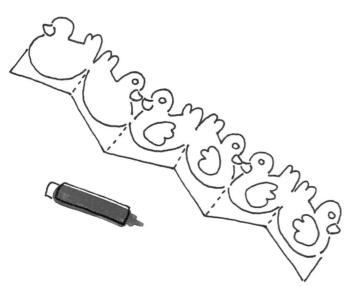

EASTER HOLIDAY

3 Open out the concertina. You will have 6 duckling silhouettes. Draw in their wings, eyes and *beaks* to match the duckling you drew.

4 Colour the ducklings and their pond with paints or felt pens. Try painting alternate ducklings in different colours.

'RATTLE AND ROLL' PUZZLE

you will need...

For the Easter Egg Puzzle

Round cheese box with clear plastic lid
Polystyrene or frozen pizza backing
Paints
Paintbrushes
Felt tip pens
5 dried peas or beans
Narrow ribbon, about 25 cm (10 in)
Sticky tape or cling film
Pencil
Scissors

Have fun decorating the lid and box with paints or felt tip pens.

Shake the puzzle and try to get all the peas into the bunnies' eyes at the same time.

If your cheese box has a cardboard lid, cut out a circle from the middle and stretch a piece of cling film across the gap - now you can see inside without losing the peas!

Put the same number of peas into the box as there are holes.

making an Easter puzzle...

Easter Egg

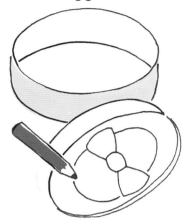

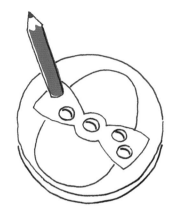

1   Take the card disc out of the base of the box. Draw round it to make a disc from polystyrene. Draw an Easter egg and bow on the polystyrene.

2   Mark the position of 5 holes in the bow. Push the end of the pencil into the polystyrene, hard enough to make a dent at each mark. (You do not need to make an actual hole.)

3   Decorate the box, inside and out, with paint or felt pens. Decorate the lid too.

4   Paint the Easter egg and bow in bright colours on the polystyrene disc. Put the card disc and then the painted disc back in the box.

5   Put 5 dried peas into the box. Put the lid on and seal it with sticky tape or cling wrap.

6   Make a small ribbon bow. Glue it to the side of the box.

EASTER HOLIDAY

81

SALT DOUGH EASTER TREE

you will need...

Cardboard scrap

Salt dough (see page 252)

Twiggy branch

Plant pot

Broad ribbon, about 1 m (1 yd)

Small pebbles, enough to fill
the plant pot

Embroidery thread
or narrow ribbon,
about 1 m (1 yd)

Paints

Paintbrushes

Rolling pin

Knife

Skewer

Pencil

Scissors

82

The number of eggs you
need will depend on the size of the branch
you have chosen, and the size of the
eggs you make.

Experiment
with different
designs and
colours.

You may need to
glue the ribbon to
the pot, to stop it
slipping down.

Pack the
pebbles all
around the
stem of the
branch, making
sure it stands
upright.

making an Easter tree...

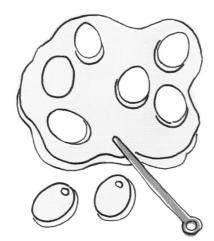

1 Draw an egg shape on the cardboard in pencil. Cut it out.

2 Roll out the salt dough to a thickness of about 0.5 cm (1/8 in). Cut round the cardboard egg to make egg shapes from dough. Make a hole in each egg with a skewer. Bake the eggs (see page 252).

3 When the dough eggs are cool, paint them in pastel colours on both sides. Allow the paint to dry.

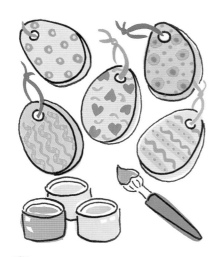

4 Paint on wavy lines, dots, stars and hearts in contrasting colours. Thread a piece of embroidery thread or ribbon through each hole and make a loop.

5 Paint the twiggy branch pale blue. You may need to give it more than one coat.

6 Paint the pot yellow. Tie ribbon round it and make a bow. Pack pebbles round the branch to keep it upright. Hang the eggs from the tree.

ROYAL EGGS

The Queen's earrings are made by threading beads and a sequin onto thread, then gluing the free end of the thread to the egg.

The shape of the crown is up to you - here are some designs you might like to copy.

Wool or raffia, cut into short pieces, makes good hair.

Cover the head with gummed coloured paper, glue on a pair of tiny wool plaits and finish with pretty ribbon bows.

you will need...

For the King
Egg, hardboiled
Cardboard tube, about 3 cm
(1¼ in) long
Gold paper, a strip about
4 x 15 cm (1½ x 6 in)

Black tissue paper, narrow strips
Paints + paintbrushes
Felt tip pens
Round stickers, sequins
Scissors
Glue or sticky tape

making a royal egg...

King

1 Paint the cardboard tube to look like a collar. Sit the egg on it when it is dry.

2 Stick on round stickers for eyes, and draw in a nose and cheeks with felt pen.

3 Glue tissue paper strips onto the head for hair. Glue a fringe of shorter tissue strips below the nose for a moustache.

4 Cut a crown from gold paper. Decorate it with sequins and stickers. Tape the ends together to fit round the head and glue or tape it on the egg.

DECORATED EGGS

To spray a fine mist of paint onto the egg, draw your finger gently across the toothbrush bristles.

Stamp dots at random, or make a formal pattern.

Paste on different colours of tissue to create an interesting, layered effect.

Paste a deep pink tissue heart onto a pale pink tissue-covered egg and give it as a gift to someone you love.

you will need...

For the Speckled Egg
Egg, hardboiled
Paints + paintbrushes
Old toothbrush
Newspapers

For the Spotted Egg
Egg, hardboiled
Paints + paintbrushes
Pencil, with eraser tip

For the Tissue Paper Egg
Egg, hardboiled
Coloured tissue paper
Paintbrush
Glue, diluted with water

making the decorated eggs...

Speckled

![1] Cover your work area with newspapers, or work outside. Paint the egg.

![2] Dip the toothbrush into paint of a contrasting colour. Splatter the egg with paint by drawing your finger across the bristles.

Spotted

![1] Paint the egg, covering it completely.

![2] Dip the eraser tip of the pencil into paint of a contrasting colour. Stamp dots of paint in a pattern or at random all over the egg.

Tissue Paper

![1] Cut different coloured tissue paper into lots of little triangles.

![2] Paste the triangles onto the egg using the dilute glue and a paintbrush. Build up layers of tissue until the whole egg is covered.

EASTER BONNETS

you will need...

For the Chicks Bonnet

Cardboard, scrap

Green card, about 45 cm (18 in) square

Red card, about 20 cm (8 in) square

Green crepe paper, about 20 cm (8 in) square

Ribbon, two pieces each about 35 cm (13½ in) long

A ball of yellow wool

Round blue stickers

Black felt tip pen

Stapler or sticky tape

Scissors

Glue

Glue the feet on at different angles to make the chicks more fun.

For the Bunnies bonnet, glue a trio of grey rabbits – trace these if you like – around the brim of a cone made from blue card.

The whiskers, noses and inner ears are made from crepe paper.

COOL STUFF

88

making an Easter bonnet...

Chicks

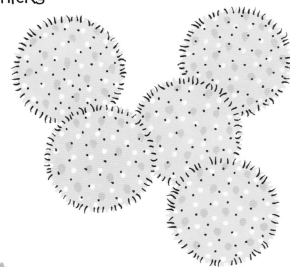

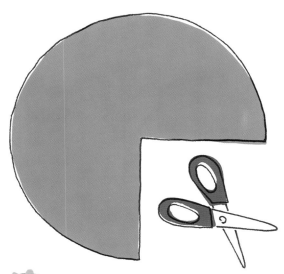

1 Make 5 yellow pompoms (see page 250 for instructions). Make 10 pompoms if you want chicks at the back of the bonnet too.

2 Make a cone from a circle of green card the size of a dinner plate (see page 246). Tape or staple the cone in shape.

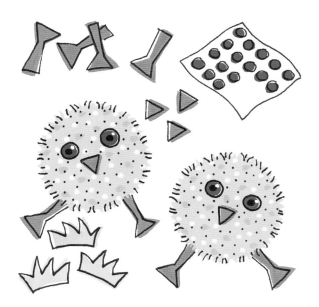

3 Cut 2 feet and 1 beak from red card for each chick (copy the ones above). Glue them on the chicks, and add stickers for eyes. Cut zigzag tufts of grass from crepe paper.

4 Glue the chicks onto the bonnet. Glue the grass in the spaces between the chicks. Staple a ribbon inside the bonnet on each side. Tie the ribbon under your chin.

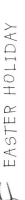

89

PARTY TIME
Hallowe'en

Spooky Lanterns

Hallowe'en Mobile

Jiggly Skeleton

Trick or Treat
Party Bags

Jack-o'-lantern

Leafy Monsters

91

SPOOKY LANTERNS

you will need...

For the Cat Lantern

Glass jar

Orange + yellow tissue paper, torn
    into strips

Black paper, about 10 cm (4 in) square

String, raffia or cord, about 1 m (1 yd)

2 beads

Pencil

Paintbrush

Small candle
    or tea light

Scissors

Glue, diluted
    with water

You can use any colour of tissue paper for these lanterns, but cut the silhouettes out of black paper for the spookiest results!

Capture your own midnight sky with this lantern – cover the jar with dark blue and black tissue, glue on a sleepy crescent moon, and finish with a sprinkling of sticker stars.

Cut these creepy spiders out of black paper and make them scuttle in all directions over your jar.

making a spooky lantern...

Cat

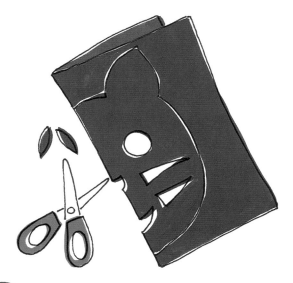

1 Paste tissue strips onto the jar using dilute glue and a paintbrush. Cover the jar completely.

2 Fold the *black* paper in half. Draw half a cat's face next to the fold (copy the picture above). Cut out eyes, nose, mouth and whiskers and cut around the head. Cut 2 pupils.

3 Glue the cat face and pupils onto the jar. Knot a bead onto each end of a 75 cm (30 in) piece of string. Tie the shorter piece of string around the top of the jar, catching in the beaded ends of the longer piece.

4 Put a small candle or tea light into the jar. Use the long, *beaded* string to carry the lantern, or to hang it from a branch.

HALLOWE'EN MOBILE

you will need...

Cardboard box
Newspaper, torn into strips
Red, black + orange paper,
    small sheets
Paints
Paintbrushes
Felt tip pens
Bristles, from an old brush
Wool or thread, 5 lengths each about
    15 cm (6 in)
Round blue + star stickers
2 small beads
2 small buttons
Darning needle
Pencil
Scissors
Glue
Glue, diluted with water

You may prefer to sew on the Cat's button eyes and mouth.

Hang the mobile from a loop of wool.

The Bat's inner ears and the Hat's crescent moon are cut from orange paper and glued in place.

Add details with felt tip pens.

Make the Spider's legs extra long and creepy.

making a Hallowe'en mobile...

1 Cut a cat, bat, pump-kin, witch's hat and spider out of cardboard (trace the ones opposite).

2 Paste newspaper strips onto the shapes using a paintbrush and dilute glue (see page 245). Allow to dry.

3 Paint all the shapes white. Allow to dry. Then paint the cat and spider black, the bat grey, the hat purple, and the pumpkin orange/green.

4 Glue on the cat's but-ton eyes, bristle whiskers and red paper nose and inner ears. Glue black paper cut outs on the pumpkin. Glue bristle whiskers on the bat and add sticker eyes.

5 Stick star stickers and a paper moon on the hat. The spider's eyes are glued-on beads. For legs, fold 4 long strips of black paper con-certina-style and glue the mid-dle of each strip to the body.

6 Thread the needle with a length of wool and link the top of the spider with the bottom of the hat. Link the hat and pumpkin with another length of wool, and so on. Tie the top length in a loop.

95

JIGGLY SKELETON

you will need...

White card, 2 large sheets

White wax crayon or candle

Black paint or ink

Paintbrush

13 paper fasteners

Wool or string, about 30 cm (12 in)

Darning needle

Pencil

Scissors

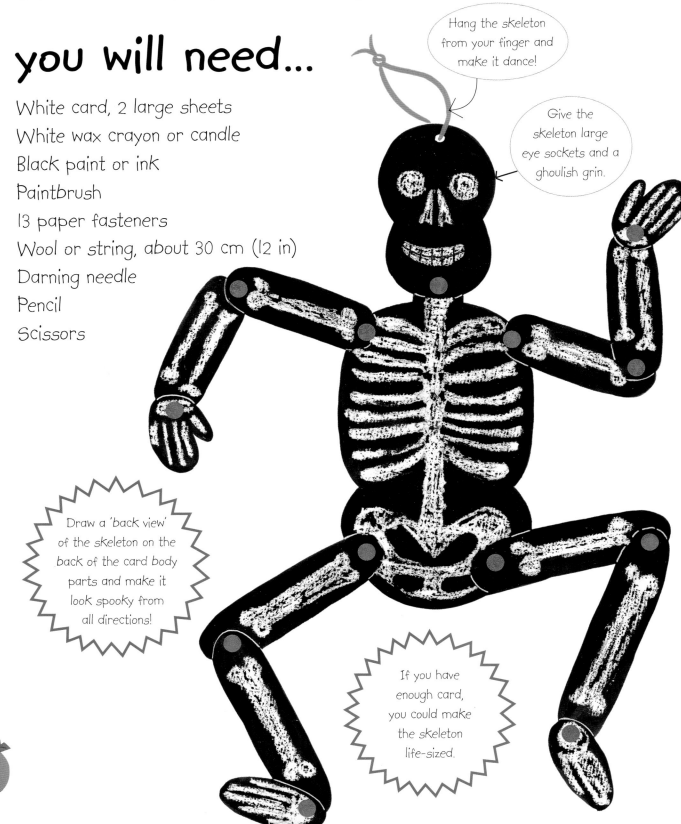

Hang the skeleton from your finger and make it dance!

Give the skeleton large eye sockets and a ghoulish grin.

Draw a 'back view' of the skeleton on the back of the card body parts and make it look spooky from all directions!

If you have enough card, you could make the skeleton life-sized.

making a jiggly skeleton...

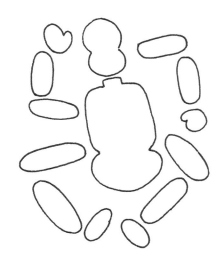

1 Draw body parts in pencil on white card (trace the *skeleton* opposite). You need 1 head, 1 body, 4 arm parts, 2 hands, 4 leg parts, and 2 feet. Cut out.

2 Copying the picture on page 96, draw the outline of bones, eye sockets and a mouth in pencil. Fill in the outlines with crayon.

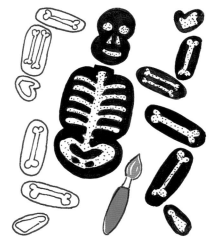

3 Paint all the card pieces black. (The crayon will not take the paint and so the white bones of the *skeleton* will show through.)

4 Lay the *skeleton* out so that the head, arms, legs, hands and feet are in place. Punch a hole with the needle through both layers where the pieces overlap.

5 Push a paper fastener through each hole and open it out at the back.

6 Thread the needle with wool and punch a hole at the top of the *skull*. Make a loop with the wool and tie the ends so that you can hang the *skeleton* up.

TRICK OR TREAT PARTY BAGS

For the Witch's Hat bag, glue two pieces together and decorate with sparkly star stickers.

The Cat has black-on-yellow sticker eyes and frayed crepe paper whiskers glued on either side of a painted nose.

you will need...

For the Pumpkin Bag

Orange crepe paper, about 20 x 30 cm (8 x 12 in)

Green crepe paper, about 30 cm (12 in) square

Black crepe paper, about 5 x 10 cm (2 x 4 in)

Raffia, 2 lengths each about 40 cm (16 in)

4 square or round stickers, or small pieces of sticky tape

Pencil

Hole punch

Scissors

Glue

Make sure you strengthen the holes for the handles with stickers or pieces of sticky tape, otherwise the bag will tear as you fill it with sweets.

making a party bag...

Pumpkin

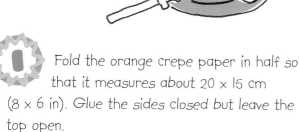

1 Fold the orange crepe paper in half so that it measures about 20 x 15 cm (8 x 6 in). Glue the sides closed but leave the top open.

2 Cut out 2 sets of 2 leaves and a stalk from green paper (trace the picture on page 98). Glue a set of leaves to the top edge of the bag, front and back.

3 From black paper, cut 3 triangles for the eyes and nose, and a row of teeth (copy the ones in the picture if you need to). Glue them on the front of the bag.

4 On the inside of the bag, put a sticker where you will make holes for the handles. Punch the holes (4 in all). Thread raffia handles through the holes and knot on the outside.

JACK-O'-LANTERN

you will need...

For the Pumpkin Face

Pumpkin

Craft knife (*be careful!*)

Spoon

Pencil

Whole cloves

Dried orange slices
   (*see page 246*)

Metal skewer

Wool or twine,
   about 1.5 m (1½ yd)

Darning needle

Tea light or
   night light or
   candle

Cut slices of orange in advance and dry them slowly in a cool oven or over a radiator.

Make sure the earrings dangle on a level with the cheeks.

For a really different lantern, let candlelight shine out through stars, moons and tiny holes cut out all round the pumpkin.

making a jack-o'-lantern...

Face

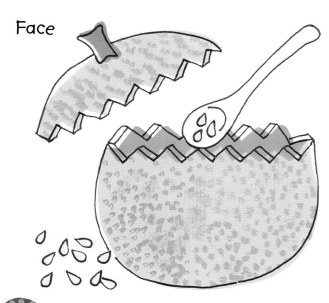

1   Cut a zigzag around the top of the pumpkin with the craft knife (an adult should help you), and put this lid to one side. Scoop out the flesh and seeds of the pumpkin. Do not make the shell too thin.

2   Draw eyes, nose, mouth and star cheeks on the front of the pumpkin in pencil. Cut out the eyes, nose and mouth with the craft knife (an adult should help you). Press cloves into the cheeks.

3   Push 2 holes in each side of the pumpkin with a skewer. With the needle, thread each orange slice onto a 30 cm (12 in) piece of wool. Tie each on the inside of the pumpkin, leaving the orange earring to dangle.

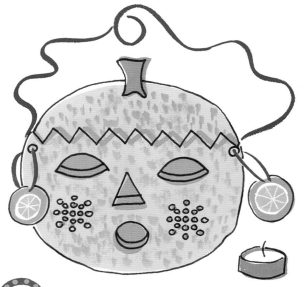

4   To make a handle, tie each end of a 75 cm (30 in) length of wool to the sides of the pumpkin, using the earring holes. Put the tea light inside the pumpkin and replace the lid.

HALLOWE'EN

101

LEAFY MONSTERS

you will need...

Assorted leaves in autumn colours

Dark paper, a large sheet

Dried pulses (lentils, peas)
  or popcorn kernels

Straw

Old telephone directory

Some heavy books

Scissors

Glue

Use your imagination and create some weird and wonderful new creatures!

This bloated beastie has long leaf legs, straw arms, frazzled ferny hair and a large red leaf for a mouth.

A snake with legs? A lizard with hair? Make this fierce monster from a variety of brightly-coloured leaves, carefully matched for size.

Choose a dark colour for your background paper to show the monsters off at their best

making a leafy monster...

1 Collect leaves in as many colours, shapes and sizes as you can.

2 Press the leaves immediately by placing them between the pages of the telephone directory. Shut the directory and put some heavy books on top, to add weight. Leave them for two weeks.

3 Arrange the leaves on backing paper. Make monsters, insects and weird animals using different leaves for bodies, legs, ears, hands and antennae. Use pulses for eyes.

4 When you are happy with your creatures, glue the leaves in place on the paper.

PARTY TIME
Christmas fun

Candy Wreath

Christmas Stocking

Tree Fairy

Fingerprint Robin
Cards + Tags

Painted Pasta
Garland + Star

Raffia Reindeer
+ Straw Star

Potato Stamp
Gift Wrap

CANDY WREATH

you will need...

Green card, about 40 cm (16 in)
   square
Yellow card, a large sheet
Small sprigs of spruce, enough to fill
   a carrier bag
Assorted coloured paper, scraps
Double-sided tape
Darning needle
Red wool
Cup, about 9 cm (3½ in) in
   diameter
Cup, about 6 cm
   (2³⁄₈ in) in diameter
2 sizes of
   dinner plate
13 wrapped sweets
Broad red ribbon,
   about 1 m (1 yd)
Scissors
Glue

You can look forward to eating the candy on the twelfth day of Christmas, when you take down the wreath and other decorations.

Give the sweet wrappers extra sparkle using a gold or silver marker pen.

An easy way to make a star is to glue together 2 paper squares so that the corners make the eight points of a star.

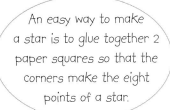

If you don't have spruce, any evergreen will do; or you can glue on leaves cut from green crepe paper.

making a candy wreath...

1 Cut a large ring from green card, using 2 sizes of plates to draw around. Glue sprigs of spruce onto one side of the ring, to completely cover it.

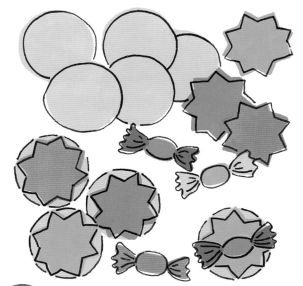

2 Cut 12 small circles and one large circle from yellow card, using the 2 cups to draw around. Cut stars from paper. Glue a star to each circle and tape a sweet on top.

3 Using the needle threaded with wool, make a hole in each yellow card bauble. Tie baubles all the way round the wreath, and finish each with a neat bow.

4 Tie the large bauble from the top of the wreath, so that it hangs in the open centre. Hang the wreath from ribbon looped around the top of the wreath and tied in a bow.

107

CHRISTMAS STOCKING
you will need...

Blue, green, red, yellow, white +
  orange felt, scraps
Fabric scraps in bright colours,
  tartans or checks
Red + green braid ('ric-rac') or
  ribbon, scraps
Assorted small buttons
Red + green wool, scraps
Embroidery thread
Sewing thread
Pins
Needles
Pinking shears
Scissors
Fabric glue

Hang your stocking up on Christmas Eve using a loop of braid sewn inside the top of the stocking.

Glue a wool fringe onto the scarf, then sew or glue the snowman's eyes, buttons, scarf and pompom in place.

Your neat stitches in bright-coloured thread will be part of the decoration.

Glue a pile of felt snowballs near the base of the snowman.

Cut around the stocking with pinking shears to prevent the edges fraying.

making a Christmas stocking...

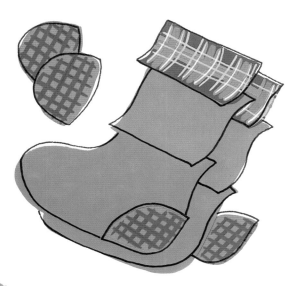

1 Cut out the pieces for 2 stocking shapes from the coloured felt and fabric (trace the stocking on page 254). Cut an extra toe and heel from fabric.

2 Glue (or pin, tack and then sew) the pieces together to make 2 stocking shapes. Glue on the toes and heels. Glue or sew on braid or ribbon for decoration.

3 From felt, cut a snowman and snowballs (white), scarf (red), hat (yellow) and carrot nose (orange) – trace the picture on page 108. Glue or sew the snowman and snowballs to the front of the stocking. Make a scarf fringe and pompom (see page 250) from wool. Embroider white snowflakes (see page 247).

4 Pin the 2 stocking pieces together, right sides out. Trim the edges with pinking shears. Sew the pieces together using a simple running stitch (see page 247), leaving the top open. Sew a loop of braid inside the top of the stocking so that you can hang it up.

TREE FAIRY
you will need...

Thin coloured card, about 40 cm
   (16 in) square
Coloured paper, a small sheet
Silver card, about 15 x 30 cm
  . (6 x 12 in)
4 lolly sticks
Assorted tiny beads or
   buttons + sequins
Star stickers
Yellow, orange or brown
   tissue paper, thin
   strips
Felt scrap
Cocktail stick
Dinner plate
Gold thread
Embroidery thread
Embroidery needle
Felt tip pens
Sticky tape
Scissors
Pinking shears
Glue

Glue the wand onto
the lolly stick hand.

You can sew the
button eyes onto the
card face if you wish.

Make the fairy's
dress and wings
sparkle with lots of
shiny stars and
sequins.

Stitch a short piece of paper string to
the shoe, and unravel both ends to make a
different kind of bow.

making a tree fairy...

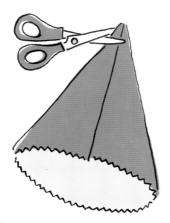

1 Cut a semicircle from card with pinking shears (draw round a dinner plate). Make the semicircle into a cone (see page 246) and tape to hold. Cut the top off the cone.

2 Cover 2 lolly stick arms with folded coloured paper to make the sleeves, leaving the hands peeking out. Glue the arms onto the back of the cone.

3 Fold the silver card in half. Draw a wing on the card, cut it out and open. You will have a pair of wings joined in the middle. Decorate with stars and sequins. Glue to the back of the cone.

4 Cut a head and neck from card (copy the picture above). Draw on a nose and mouth. Glue on bead or button eyes, and tissue paper hair. Thread beads or sequins together for a halo and glue in place. Tape the neck inside the cone.

5 Decorate 2 lolly stick legs with felt pens. Glue on 2 felt shoes (copy the shoes on page 110). For the bows, make a stitch with embroidery thread, knot the ends and fray. Glue the legs inside the front of the cone.

6 For the fairy's wand, glue one end of a length of gold thread to the tip of the cocktail stick. Wind the thread up the stick, covering it. Glue a star or sequin to the top. Decorate the fairy's dress with sequins and stars.

FINGERPRINT ROBIN CARDS + TAGS

you will need...

For the Robin Cards

White + red thin card, large sheets

Green paper, small sheet

Black felt tip pen

Red + brown paints

Red + green round stickers

Scissors

Pinking shears

Glue

For the Robin Tags

White + green thin card, large sheets

Red + green embroidery thread

Red + green round stickers

Red + green coloured paper

Red + brown paints

Hole punch

Scissors

Pinking shears

Glue

Cut strips of coloured paper with pinking shears and glue them as a frame around a group of robins.

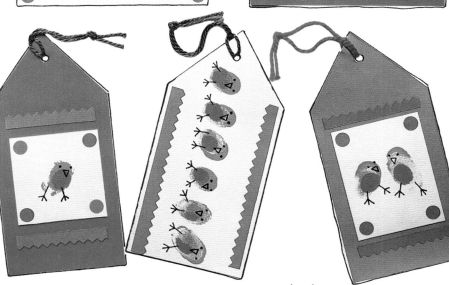

Print the robins at random - some standing alone, some in pairs, and some in groups.

Don't try to make all the robins the same - instead draw their beaks and legs facing different ways, and make each one unique!

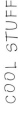

COOL STUFF

making a robin card + tag...

Card

1 Dip your index finger into the brown paint and print a robin body onto a large sheet of white card. Dip your little finger in red paint and print a red breast slightly overlapping the body. Print lots of robins.

2 Draw in a *beak*, 2 eyes and 2 legs on each robin with *black felt* pen.

Tag

3 Cut and fold the white card to make a Christmas card, or cut out a robin and glue it to a folded piece of red card. Decorate with *stickers* and *coloured paper* shapes.

1 Make robins as in Steps 1 and 2 above. Cut tags from the printed white card, or cut out a group of robins and glue onto a tag cut from green card. Decorate the tags with stickers and coloured paper. Loop thread through a hole punched in the tag.

PAINTED PASTA GARLAND + STAR

you will need...

For the Garland

Pasta tubes suitable for threading

Paints

Paintbrushes

Felt tip pens

Wool or embroidery
   thread in bright
   colours

Stiff card, about
   3 x 7 cm
   (1¼ x 2¾ in)

Darning needle

Scissors

For the Star

8 pasta tubes

Thin coloured card, about
   5 cm (6 in) square

Wool, about 20 cm (8 in)

Paints

Paintbrushes

Button

Scissors

Glue

You can make this garland as long
as you like – just keep threading pasta
and tying tassels!

Hang
the star from a
loop of wool.

When you have finished your
garland, tie the wool ends together
or tie each one around the last
pasta shape.

COOL STUFF

114

making a garland + star...

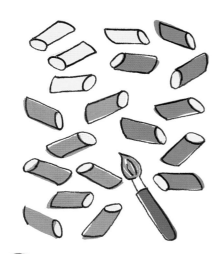

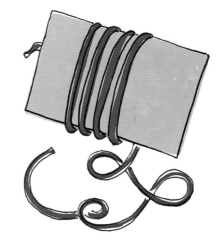

1 Paint half the pasta tubes red and half green. Allow to dry.

2 Decorate the pasta with spots, wavy lines, zigzags and stripes, using paints or felt pens.

3 For the tassels, wind wool 4 times round the card. Cut off the extra wool.

Star

4 Thread the needle with another length of wool and push it between the card and the wool wound onto it. Repeat and pull this stitch tight. Knot the wool close to the card, leaving long ends. Cut the wool along the bottom edge of the card (see page 249).

5 Thread the pasta tubes and tie the tassels onto a long length of wool. Alternate the red and green pasta tubes and tie a tassel between each pair of pasta tubes.

6 Decorate the pasta as in Steps 1 and 2 above. Glue the pasta onto the card to form a star shape. Glue the button in the centre. Trim the card around the star. Glue a loop of wool to the back of the card to hang it up with.

115

RAFFIA REINDEER + STRAW STAR

The straw star makes a simple decoration which will look festive on the Christmas tree, or hanging from a picture frame or doorway.

Try and match the twigs for size, shape and number of branches.

Why not make a whole team of reindeer, linked with thread harnesses, and then start on a sled?

Bend the neck, head and tail into shape to give your reindeer personality!

you will need...

You may have to adjust the legs a little at first, but then the reindeer should stand without support.

COOL STUFF

For the Raffia Reindeer
Natural raffia
Narrow cardboard tube
4 pipe cleaners
Red embroidery thread
2 branched twigs of similar size
Sticky tape (optional)
Scissors
Glue

For the Straw Star
Straw, 4 lengths each about 6 cm (2³⁄₈ in)
Red embroidery thread
Scissors

making a reindeer + star...

Reindeer

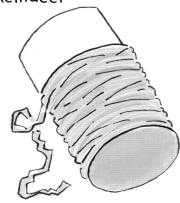

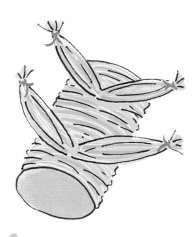

Dotted red line indicates the pipe cleaner beneath the raffia.

1 Wind the raffia around the cardboard tube to completely cover it, gluing the raffia on as you go.

2 For the legs, tie lengths of raffia to both ends of 2 pipe cleaners with thread. Make sure the pipe cleaners are completely covered. Fold each in half. Glue the folds to the tube, front and back.

3 Cover another pipe cleaner with raffia. Fold the bundle in half - the fold will be the nose. Bend to make a head and neck. Tie thread around the nose and the top of the neck. Glue the base of the neck to the tube.

Straw Star

4 Cut a pipe cleaner in half. Bundle raffia around one half and tie both ends with thread. Glue one end to the end of the body to make a tail.

5 Glue on twig antlers. Stuff the tube with raffia to finish the body.

1 Make a cross with 2 pieces of straw and tie it at the centre with thread (do not cut the thread yet). Lay a second straw cross over the first one to form a star. Bind the crosses together and make a loop of thread to hang the star up with.

117

POTATO STAMP GIFT WRAP

To get a clear print, press the potato print down cleanly – try not to move it! – and then carefully lift it off.

Print a star made from a freehand drawing for a real handmade look – or design a print of your own.

These Christmas trees are printed in two stages – first the green tree shape, and then the red rectangle for the pot.

The blue dots are printed with a pencil eraser tip dipped in blue paint.

COOL STUFF

you will need...

For the Star Gift Wrap

Potato, cut in half

White or coloured paper, a large sheet

Red + green paint + paintbrushes

Pencil, with eraser tip

Tracing paper

Craft Knife (be careful!)

Pins

Scissors

making the gift wrap...

Star

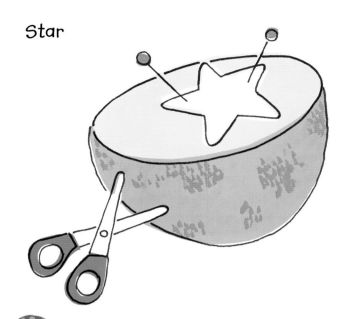

① On paper, draw a star. Cut out. Pin the paper star to one half of the potato.

② Cut around the star with a craft knife (an adult should help you with this) about 0.5 cm (1/4 in) deep. Cut away the potato around the star.

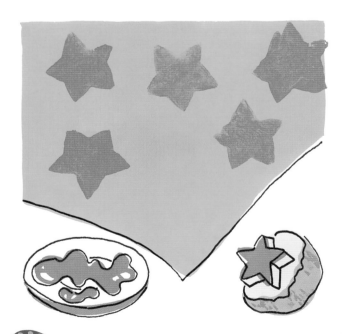

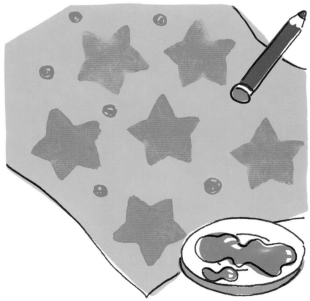

③ Dip the star into the red paint and print 3 or 4 star shapes onto the wrapping paper. Repeat until you have printed stars all over the paper.

④ Dip the eraser tip of the pencil in green paint and print dots between the stars, all over the paper. Dip the pencil in the paint after every 3 or 4 prints.

119

RAINY DAY
fun with paper

Panda Paper Doll

Curled Paper
Animals

Car Collage
Pinboard

Pencil Holders

Fruity Picture
Frames

PANDA PAPER DOLL

you will need...

Thin card, a large sheet
Cardboard box lid, shoe box-sized
   or smaller
Paper, a large sheet
Paints
Paintbrushes
Felt tip pens
Round blue
   stickers
Sticky tape
Scissors
Glue

Trace this Panda, or make yours bigger – just be sure the clothes you make fit him!

Don't forget to include tabs with every item of clothing.

making a panda paper doll...

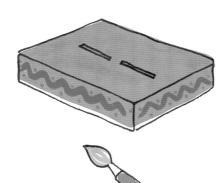

1 Draw a Panda on card (trace the one opposite), making 2 tabs extend below the feet. Paint it black and white. Add stickers for eyes. Cut it out.

2 Cut 2 slits in the box lid to match the position of the feet. Decorate the lid with paint or felt pen.

3 Push the tabs on the feet through the slits in the lid. Fold them *back* under the lid and glue or tape them down. The Panda should now stand upright.

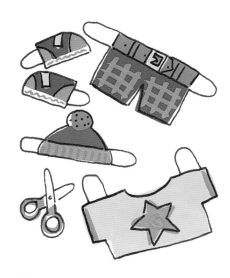

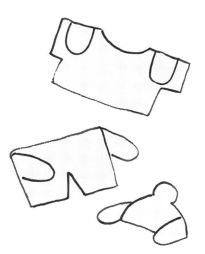

4 Draw Panda's clothes on paper (or trace the ones opposite). Remember the tabs! Paint the clothes or use felt pen, and cut out.

5 Fold the tabs back where they join the clothes (see picture above).

6 Dress the Panda in a whole wardrobe of outfits by folding the tabs behind the body to hold the clothes in place.

FUN WITH PAPER

123

CURLED PAPER ANIMALS

Starting at the back, overlap black-and-white zigzag tissue strips as spines.

The Hedgehog's feet are cut out and glued on separately.

Make Squirrel's tail really bushy by covering the paper tail with lots of tissue curls.

Add nose, ear, arm and leg details with felt pen.

you will need...

COOL STUFF

124

For the Squirrel

Thin coloured card, a large sheet

Brown paper, about 25 x 30 cm
  (10 x 12 in)

Paints + paintbrushes

Red, brown, yellow + green tissue
  paper

Felt tip pens

Pencil

Ruler

Scissors

Pinking shears

Glue

making a paper animal...

Squirrel

1 Cut out a squirrel from paper using pinking shears for the back and tail. Glue onto card. Add a nose and eye with felt pen.

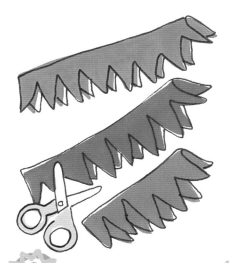

2 Cut strips of red and brown tissue, each about 7 x 20 cm ($2^{3}/_{4}$ x 8 in). Fold the strips in half, lengthways. Cut a zigzag down one long edge.

3 To make curls, pull each point on the strips of tissue paper firmly between your thumb and the edge of the ruler. Cut the strips into small pieces.

4 Glue the tissue curls onto the tail, mixing the reds and browns. Glue on narrow strips of yellow tissue paper for whiskers.

5 Glue on a ball of tissue for an eye, and another for an acorn. Cut oak leaf shapes from green tissue and glue in place.

Hedgehog

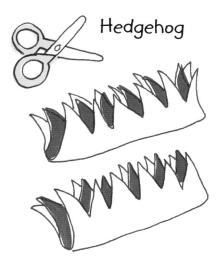

1 The Hedgehog's spines are made from strips of black and white tissue paper, folded together and cut into zigzags down one long edge.

CAR COLLAGE PINBOARD

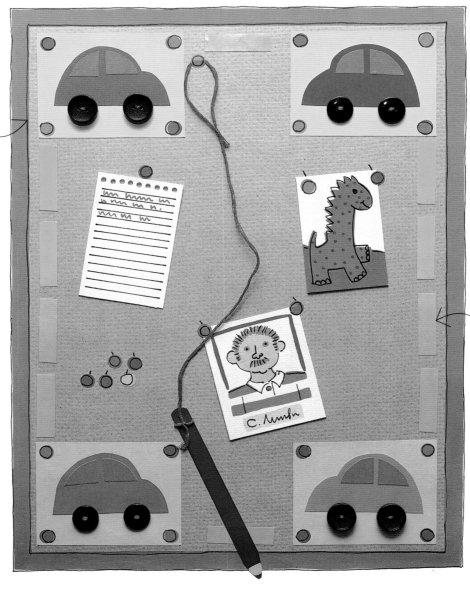

Stick the cars onto the card so that 2 are facing one way, and 2 the other.

The strips of yellow paper look like road markings.

you will need...

Cork pinboard

Thin card, about 20 x 30 cm
   (8 x 12 in)

Blue + yellow paper, small sheets

Assorted coloured paper, small sheets

Drawing pins

8 buttons

String, about the length of the
   pinboard

Small notebook + pencil

Scissors

Glue

making a collage pinboard...

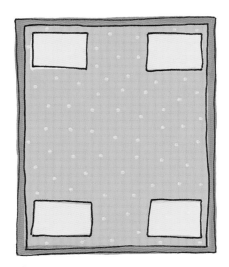

1 Cut the thin card into 4 pieces, each measuring about 10 x 15 cm (4 x 6 in). Glue one in each corner of the pinboard.

2 Cut out 4 paper cars, each a different colour. Glue a car on each piece of card. Stick 2 blue paper windows on each car.

3 Glue or sew 2 button wheels onto each car.

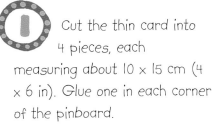

4 Pin a piece of card in each corner of the pinboard with drawing pins. Make 2 cars face one way and 2 cars the other way.

5 Cut strips of yellow paper about 1.5 cm (½ in) wide. Cut the strips into 5 cm (2 in) lengths. Glue them around the edge of the board, spacing them evenly.

6 Tie string to the end of the pencil. Make a loop in the free end of the string and pin it to the board. Pin on a notebook too.

PENCIL HOLDERS

you will need...

For the Ocean Liner Pencil Holder

3 cardboard tubes, from toilet rolls

2 cardboard boxes, one shoe box and one smaller

Dark blue paper, a small sheet

Coloured reinforcement rings or round stickers

Paints

Paintbrushes

Silver + gold foil, scraps

Wool, about 40 cm (16 in)

Sticky tape

Fabric, a scrap

Barbecue

skewer

Scissors

Glue

For this pencil holder, glue tubes of different sizes together, glue them onto a base of card, and glue on stars cut from wrapping paper.

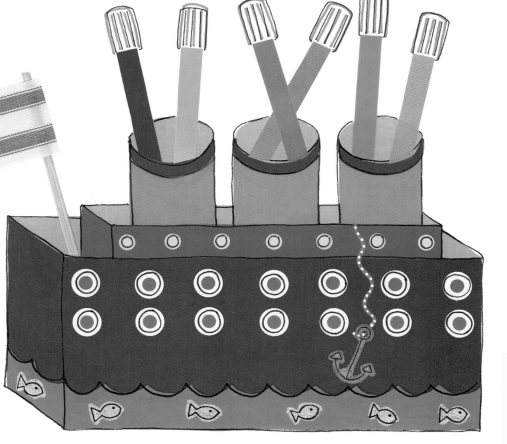

Use felt tip pens to add details to the port holes, anchor and fish.

making a pencil holder...

Ocean Liner

1 Paint the tubes red, the small box blue, and the shoe box dark blue with a wavy green sea around its base.

2 Stick rows of reinforcement rings along the sides of the boxes for port holes. Glue a band of dark blue paper around the top of each red funnel.

3 Cut fish out of silver foil, and an anchor out of gold foil. Glue the fish on below the waves. Tie wool onto the anchor. Tape the end inside the small box.

4 Tape the funnels inside the small box, then glue this box inside the shoe box. Glue a fabric flag to the top of the skewer. Tape the skewer inside the shoe box.

FUN WITH PAPER

FRUITY PICTURE FRAMES

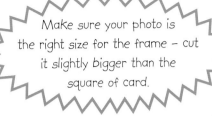

Make sure your photo is the right size for the frame – cut it slightly bigger than the square of card.

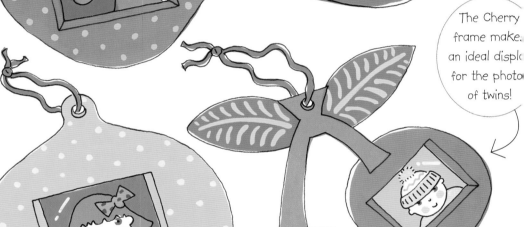

Make a fruit salad of Strawberry, Lemon and Cherry frames to display photos of family or pets.

The Cherry frame make. an ideal displo for the photo of twins!

you will need...

For the Apple Frame

Corrugated or plain cardboard, about 30 cm (12 in) square

Newspaper, cut into strips

Raffia or wool, about 30 cm (12 in)

Paints, paintbrushes + felt tip pens

Sticky tape

Scissors + hole punch

Glue, diluted with water

making a fruity frame...

Apple

1 Draw an apple shape on the cardboard. Cut it out. Cut a square out of the centre.

2 Paste newspaper strips on the apple with dilute glue and a paintbrush. Cover the whole surface and the edges. Allow to dry.

3 Punch a hole in the stalk. Paint the apple, leaves and stalk, adding leaf markings with felt pen. Remember to paint the back of the frame too.

4 Tie a loop of raffia through the hole. Place a photo in the frame. Replace the square you cut out and tape it to the frame behind the photo.

FUN WITH PAPER

131

RAINY DAY
fun with paint

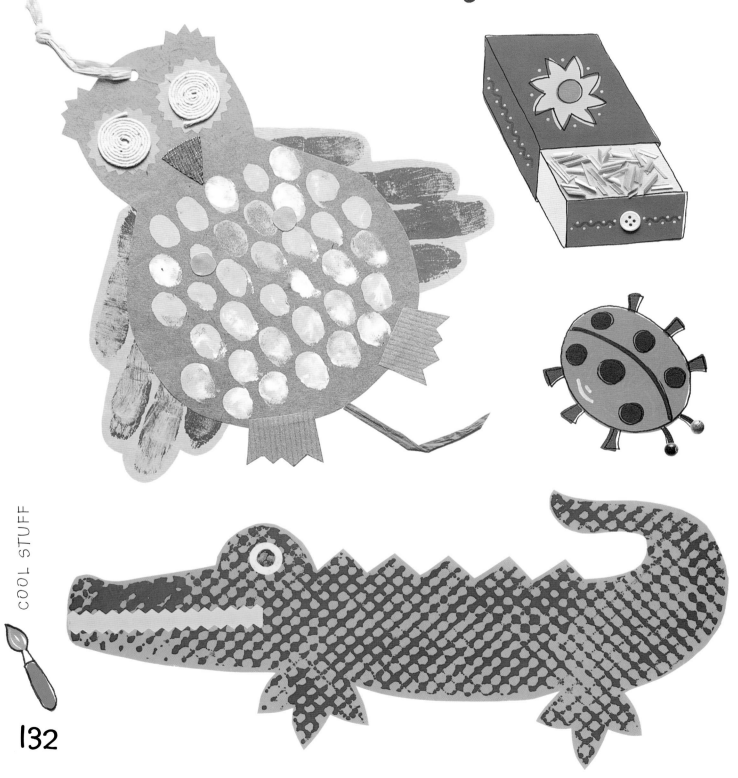

Matchbox Insect

Printed Crocodile
Family

Mosaic Plant Pots

Fingerprint Owl

Stencilled
T-Shirts

MATCHBOX INSECT

you will need...

For the Ladybird

Dark brown or black thick paper,
   a small sheet

Matchbox

Pebble, to fit inside matchbox

Paints

Paintbrushes

2 small beads

Button

Straw, a handful

Scissors

Glue

Mixing the paint with the glue makes it stick to the pebble.

Glue the legs slightly under the pebble, making sure they stick out at the sides.

Bee's wings are cut from cellophane, but you could use shiny sweet wrappers or tracing paper instead.

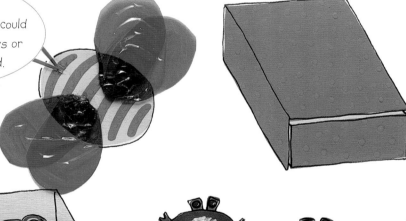

The Seashore Beasties have tiny shells glued onto their backs, and scraps of dried seaweed glued on for tails.

making a matchbox insect...

Ladybird

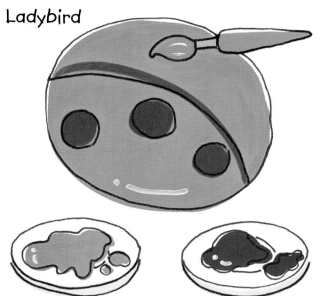

① Mix a little red and black paint with glue. Paint the pebble red. Allow to dry. Paint black spots and a black stripe down the middle.

② Cut 8 small strips of paper, each about 0.5 x 1.5 cm ($\frac{1}{8}$ x $\frac{1}{2}$ in). Glue on 6 strips for legs and 2 for the antennae. Thread or glue a bead on each antenna.

③ Paint the matchbox blue. Allow to dry. Add the flower and wavy line/dot detail.

④ Glue the button onto the drawer. Fill the drawer with straw for bedding.

FUN WITH PAINT

135

PRINTED CROCODILE FAMILY

The pattern on the polystyrene gives a realistic crocodile-skin texture.

Peel the print off slowly and carefully, trying not to smudge the paint.

you will need...

Polystyrene, or backing from
   2 large frozen pizzas
Green + yellow thin card,
   large sheets
Yellow, blue or purple paper,
   a small sheet
Green + brown paint

Paintbrushes
Craft knife (be careful!)
Round stickers
Tracing paper
Pencil, with eraser tip
Scissors + pinking shears
Glue

136

making a crocodile family...

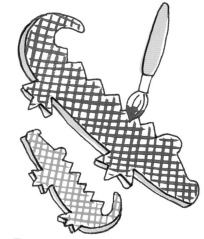

1 Trace one large and one small crocodile from the picture opposite, or draw your own.

2 Transfer the tracing onto the flat side of the polystyrene (not the patterned side). Cut out the crocodiles with a craft knife (an adult should help you).

3 Dab paint onto the patterned side of the polystyrene crocodile. Make sure the paint is sticky, and not too runny.

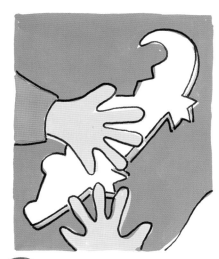

4 Press the painted side of the crocodile onto the coloured card. Press firmly with your hand – try not to move the crocodile! Carefully peel it off. Print crocodiles all over the card. Allow to dry.

5 Cut out the prints. Give each a sticker eye. Dip the eraser end of the pencil in paint and print a dot on each eye. Cut strips of paper with pinking shears and glue on for mouths.

6 To make a crocodile stand, fold a rectangle of card (copy the picture above) and glue it on the unpainted side. Fold the feet away from the body on the painted side.

FUN WITH PAINT

137

MOSAIC PLANT POTS

you will need...

For the Primula Pot

Clay plant pot

6 egg shells, crushed

Purple, light green + blue paint

Paintbrushes

Glue, diluted with water

Glue

Arrange the coloured egg shells at random, or in a simple pattern, like this one.

Choose your favourite colours, but use a dark colour for the pot, and contrasting colours for the egg shells.

Glue the egg shells close enough together to look like mosaic tiles, but leave a gap around each piece for the background colour to show through.

making a mosaic plant pot...

Primula

 1 Paint the outside of the clay pot purple. Allow to dry.

 2 Paint half the egg shell pieces green, and half blue.

3 Glue egg shell pieces all round the pot, mixing the blue and green pieces evenly. Leave gaps so that the purple shows through.

4 Paint the dilute glue all over the outside of the pot. This seals the egg shell layer and acts as a varnish.

FUN WITH PAINT

139

FINGERPRINT OWL

you will need...

Brown + yellow thin card, each
about 30 cm (12 in) square

Raffia + string, each
about 50 cm (20 in)

Pale yellow/cream +
brown paint

Paper fasteners

Brown paper + fabric
scraps

Bead

Sponge

Darning needle

Hole punch

Scissors

Pinking shears

Glue

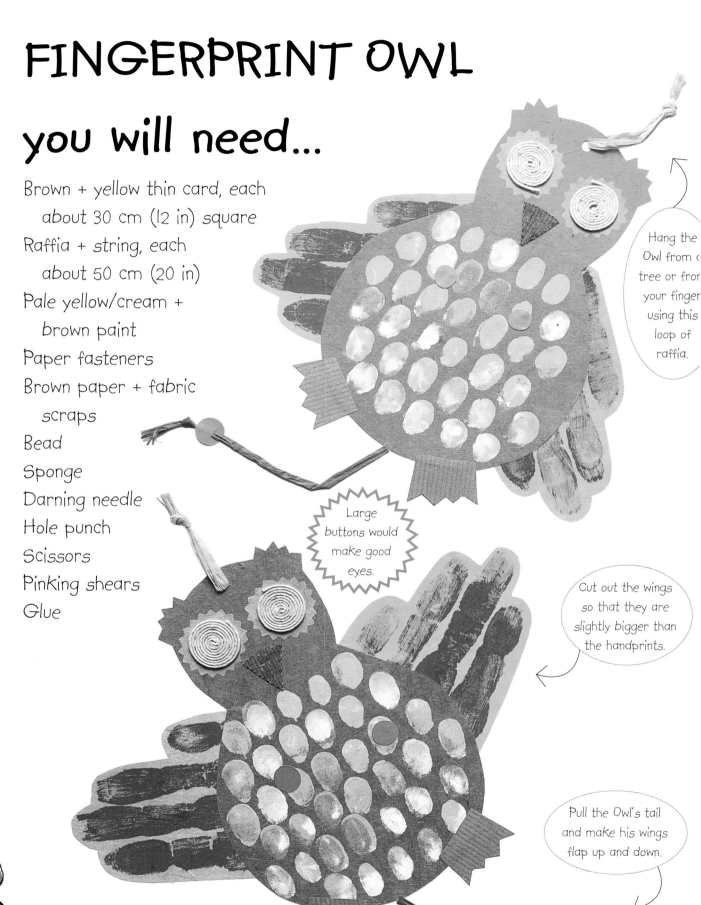

Hang the
Owl from a
tree or from
your finger
using this
loop of
raffia.

Large
buttons would
make good
eyes.

Cut out the wings
so that they are
slightly bigger than
the handprints.

Pull the Owl's tail
and make his wings
flap up and down.

making a fingerprint owl...

1 Draw an owl body on brown card. Dip your fingertip in yellow paint and make fingerprints all over the body. Cut out the body.

2 Sponge brown paint onto your hands and make prints on the yellow card. Cut around the 4 fingers of each hand print (leave off the thumb print).

3 With a needle, make 2 holes in the body and one in each wing. Fix the wings to the body with paper fasteners. Punch a hole in the top of the head and loop a piece of raffia through it.

4 Punch a hole in the top of each wing. With the wings down, loop raffia through the holes and knot it, leaving a tail dangling below the body. Knot a bead on the end of this.

5 For each eye, glue a coil of string on a 3 cm (1¼ in) square of paper. Cut round the coil with pinking shears. Glue in place.

6 Cut a beak from a scrap of fabric and 2 feet from paper (copy the picture opposite). Glue in place on the owl.

FUN WITH PAINT

141

STENCILLED T-SHIRTS

you will need...

For the Two Big Fish T-shirt

T-shirt

Thin card, about 10 x 20 cm
   (4 x 8 in)

Cardboard, about 10 x 20 cm
   (4 x 8 in)

2 small buttons or beads

Pencil, with eraser tip

Fabric paints

Sponge

Masking tape

Paper towel

Sewing thread

Needle

Scissors

Stencil a school of smaller fish in brilliant colours and brighten up a boring T-shirt.

Make sure that you place the striped stencil exactly over the fish before you begin to dab on the paint, otherwise the stripes will go beyond the outline of the fish.

Use as little paint as possible - the sponge should be almost dry - to prevent the paint creeping under the stencil and giving an untidy outline.

COOL STUFF

142

making a stencilled t-shirt...

Two Big Fish

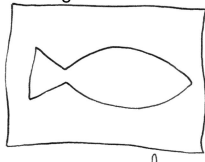

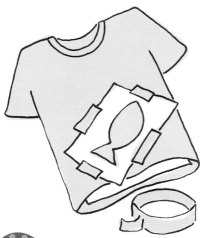

1 Draw a *big fish* on thin card. Cut out and throw away the fish shape, leaving the fish stencil (see page 251).

2 Place the stencil on the front of the T-shirt and tape it in position. Slide the cardboard inside the T-shirt, under the stencil.

3 Dip the sponge in *blue* paint and dab it onto a paper towel to remove excess paint. Dab the paint on the stencil. Allow to dry *before* carefully lifting the stencil.

4 Tape the stencil down on the T-shirt again, this time facing a different way (don't forget to move the card inside the T-shirt!). Repeat Step 3, using green paint.

5 For a striped fish, draw the fish on card as before, but cut out only the stripes. Tape this stencil over a stencilled fish. Dab on paint. For dots, dip a pencil end in paint and print.

6 Sew on buttons or beads for the eyes of both fish.

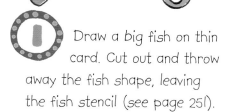

FUN WITH PAINT

143

RAINY DAY
fun with boxes

144

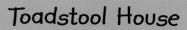
Toadstool House

Doll's House

Doll's House
Furniture

Miniature Theatre

Clothes Peg
Actors

TOADSTOOL HOUSE

you will need...

Thin card, 3 pieces:
    one about 30 cm (12 in) square
    one about 10 cm x 15 cm
    (4 x 6 in)
    one about
    15 x 75 cm
    (6 x 30 in)
Paints
Paintbrushes
Felt tip pens
Fabric scraps
Scissors
Stapler or glue

The pitch of the roof can be steep or shallow and the house tall or squat, depending on the size of the card cone and base that you make.

Glue a short length of wool one end of the spool for the mouse's tail.

Make the door big enough for the mice to go in and out.

To make a mouse, glue one end of a spool with a cut-out of a face of a mouse.

To make the feeding bowl, glue corn kernels to an upturned lid.

making a toadstool house...

1 Cut a circle from the card (draw round a dinner plate). Cut in from the edge to the centre. Paint the circle red with yellow spots. Staple or glue it into a cone shape.

2 Cut a sprig of leaves and acorns from the card (copy the picture above). Colour them with felt pens or paint. Glue the stalk inside the cone.

3 Cut the card rectangle to fit under the perimeter of the roof. Cut an arch for a door. Paint around the arch and add windows, flowers and grass.

4 Staple or glue the base of the house into a cylinder shape. Put the roof on top. Make blankets for the mice from small rectangles of fabric.

DOLL'S HOUSE

you will need...

2 cardboard boxes of equal size

Patterned wrapping paper or wallpaper

White paper, small sheets

Coloured paper, small sheets

Fabric scraps

Matchbox, outer shell

Paints

Paintbrushes

Felt tip pens

Sticky tape

Scissors

Glue

You may prefer to paint the outside of the box before you glue on the windows and door.

Make a doorknob and letter box from yellow sticker with felt pen details.

making a doll's house...

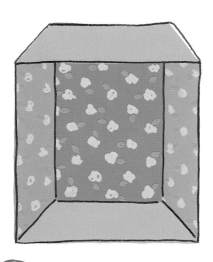

1 Cut the flaps off one box to make the house. Glue patterned paper on the walls inside.

2 Paint the ceiling (top) and floor (bottom) inside the box.

3 Draw or paint a exterior door and 2 windows on coloured paper. Cut out. Glue onto the outside of the house.

4 Draw or paint a door on coloured paper and 2 windows on white paper. Cut out. Glue scraps of fabric to the windows for curtains. Glue the windows and door inside the house.

5 Cut 2 sides off the second box, leaving a corner for the roof. Paint this red and add roof tiles with felt pen. Glue on 2 doves cut from white paper.

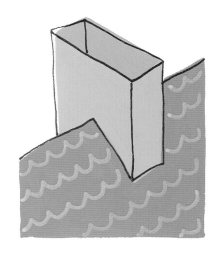

6 Paint the matchbox orange. Cut V-shaped notches in one end so that it fits on the roof as a chimney. Tape the matchbox to the roof to hold it down.

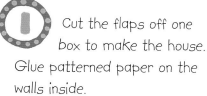

DOLL's HOUSE FURNITURE

you will need...

For the Table + Stools

2 corks, cut in half

Large empty cotton reel

Fabric scraps

Pencil

Scissors

Glue

For the Chest of Drawers

3 matchboxes

Paints + paintbrushes

3 paper fasteners

Darning
    needle

Glue

For The Mirror + Pictures

Scrap of thin card

Silver foil

Paints

Paintbrushes

Felt tip pens

Scissors

Glue

Glue the pictures and mirror to the walls of the doll' house and draw the picture wire and nail with felt pen.

For the Bookshelf

White paper, small sheet

Paints + paintbrushes

Felt tip pen.

Scissors

Glue

Draw some of the books lying down, or leaning to one side, for a realistic bookshelf.

For the Bed

Matchbox

Scrap of thin card

Paints + paintbrushes

Fabric scraps

Scissors

Glue

For the Rug

Fabric, about 5 x 11 cm
    (2 x 4½ in)

Pin

Glue

COOL STUFF

making the doll's furniture...

Table + Stools

Glue a fabric cover on the uncut end of each cork (draw round the corks for the right size). Glue a larger fabric circle to the cotton reel as a table cloth.

Chest of Drawers

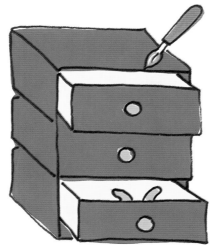

Glue the matchboxes together. Decorate with paint and felt pen. Make a hole in the centre of each drawer with the needle. Push a paper fastener through each hole and fix inside.

Mirror + Pictures

Cut an oval from card and paint it. Glue a smaller foil oval in the centre for a mirror. Draw tiny pictures on squares of card and paint frames around them.

Bookshelf

On paper, draw a shelf with books. Paint and draw in the details. Cut out and glue in position.

Bed

Cut 2 bed ends from thin card. Glue them to the ends of the matchbox. Paint the bed. Glue fabric rectangles on the bed as a pillow and blanket.

Rug

Fray the piece of fabric at both ends with a pin. Glue onto the floor of the doll's house.

MINIATURE THEATRE

you will need...

Cardboard box,
  lid flaps cut off
Thin card,
  2 pieces slightly
  smaller than the
  back of the box
4 lids or blocks,
  at least 3 cm
  (1¼ in) deep
Felt tip pens
Gold or silver
  marker pen
Paints
Paintbrushes
Gold star stickers
Gold or silver foil
Fabric scraps
2 garden canes
Sticky tape
Scissors
Glue

Make false curtains from scraps of dark fabric and glue on tiny tie-backs to keep them open.

Turn to page 154 to find out how to make these magnetic clothes peg actors.

The actors move when you slide the wooden spoons (and their magnets) about under the theatre.

The scenes are suspended from garden canes.

Draw scenes from your favourite fairy tales, or your own stories.

making a miniature theatre...

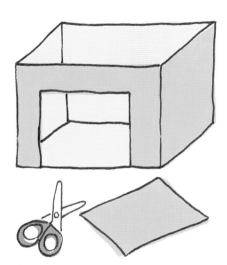

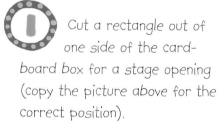

1 Cut a rectangle out of one side of the cardboard box for a stage opening (copy the picture above for the correct position).

2 Cut two V-shaped notches in the top of each side of the stage opposite each other. For the feet, glue a lid under each corner.

3 Paint the walls and floor of the theatre green. Paint the back wall dark blue, to make a night sky. Stick on star stickers and a foil moon.

4 Paint the outside of the box red and the stage opening border purple. Above the stage add a gold foil crown and detail with gold pen.

5 Glue on fabric curtains and glue on small fabric tie-backs to keep them open.

6 Draw or paint 2 scenes on the card. Glue or tape each scene to a garden cane. The canes rest on the notches cut in the sides of the box.

153

CLOTHES PEG ACTORS

you will need...

For the King, Fairy, Woman + Wolf

4 wooden clothes pegs

8 magnets

4 wooden spoons

Paints

Paintbrushes

Yellow tissue paper,
   thin strips

Brown, yellow + orange
   wool scraps

Felt tip pens

Gold marker pen

Fabric or felt scraps

Braid, sequins, star stickers

Brown paper, foil, thin card, scraps

Straw, brush bristles

Matchstick

Embroidery thread,
   needle

Hacksaw
   (be careful!)

Scissors

Glue

Glued-on bits
of unravelled string
give the Wolf's
coat a coarser
texture.

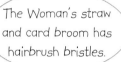

The Woman's straw
and card broom has
hairbrush bristles.

For a drawstring,
gather the long edge of
a rectangle of fabric using
an embroidery needle and
thread, ease the gathers
around the neck and tie
the thread ends
in a bow.

The Fairy's
matchstick wand
has 2 sticker stars
glued on back-
to-back.

For the King,
glue on a wool beard,
a foil crown (you can trace
this one), and a fabric
cloak fastened with
a sequin.

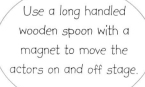

Use a long handled
wooden spoon with a
magnet to move the
actors on and off stage.

making the clothes peg actors...

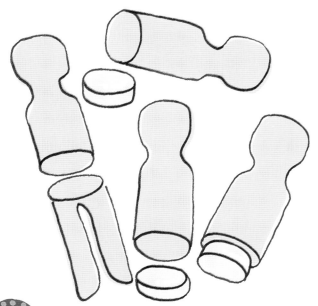

① Saw each peg in half, just above where it splits into 2 (an adult should help you with this). Glue a magnet to the base of the top half.

② For people, draw or paint faces and bodies on the pegs. Glue on wool or tissue for hair, and braid or sequins for decoration. Glue or tie on a fabric cloak or dress.

③ For the wolf, paint the peg brown. Draw eyes, nose and mouth in felt pen. Glue on brown paper ears. Glue on wisps of wool for hair and whiskers, and long strands for a tail.

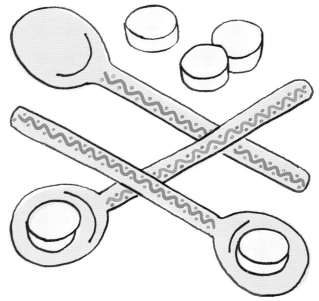

④ Glue a magnet on each spoon. Make sure it is the correct way up to attract the magnet on its peg character. Decorate the handles with felt pen.

FUN WITH BOXES

155

RAINY DAY
fun with fabric

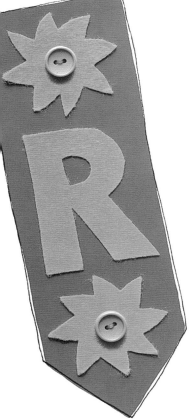

Seaside
Pin-cushions

Fat Cat Door Stop

Elephant
Wallhanging

Felt Bookmarks

Pyjama Bag

SEASIDE PIN-CUSHIONS

you will need...

For the Fish Pin-cushion

Fabric, about 25 x 30 cm
  (10 x 12 in)
Dried pulses (such as lentils) or beans
Braid ('ric-rac'), a scrap
Paper, a small sheet
2 buttons
Sewing thread
Pinking shears
Scissors
Needle
Pins

The Starfish has button eyes and a smile sewn on one side before the 2 star shapes are sewn together.

Make your stitches small and close togeth[er] to stop the pulses from escaping!

The Crab's legs and pincers are strips of fabric, caught into the stitching when the body pieces are sewn together.

making a seaside pin-cushion...

Fish

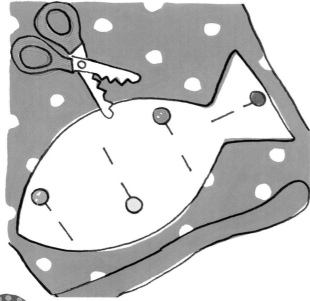

① Make a paper pattern of a fish. Fold the fabric in half and pin the paper pattern to it. Cut out round the pattern with pinking shears.

② You will have 2 fabric fish pieces. Sew a button eye on each.

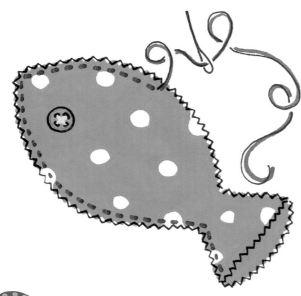

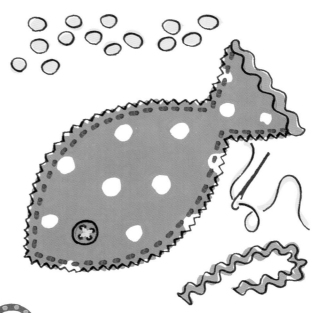

③ Pin the fish pieces together, right sides out. Sew them together using small running stitches, about 0.5 cm (1/4 in) from the edge (see page 247). Leave the tail open.

④ Stuff the fish with pulses - don't make it too full! Sew the tail closed. Sew or glue the braid on the tail for decoration.

FAT CAT DOOR STOP

you will need...

Patterned fabric, about 30 × 50 cm (12 × 20 in)

Hessian, 2 pieces 10 cm (4 in) wide × the width of a door

Broad ribbon, about 1.25 m (1¼ yd)

Kapok or old tights

Plain fabric, a scrap

Paper, a scrap

String, a scrap

Darning needle

Pins

Sewing thread

2 buttons

Pencil

Scissors

Pinking shears

To sew the mouth and whiskers in one go, start by pushing the needle into the fabric where you want one whisker, come out at the mouth, make 3 stitches, and finish by bringing the needle out at the other whisker.

Cutting the fabric with pinking shears prevents it from fraying.

Make your stitches small and close together, to stop the stuffing from leaking out.

making a fat cat door stop...

1 Make a paper pattern of a cat. Fold the fabric in half, and pin on the paper pattern. Cut out round the pattern with pinking shears.

2 On one cat shape, sew button eyes and glue on a fabric nose. Thread the darning needle with string and sew on a mouth and whiskers. Fray the ends of the whiskers.

3 Pin the 2 cat shapes together, right sides out. Sew them together using small running stitches (see page 247). Leave a small gap at the *base* for the stuffing to fit through.

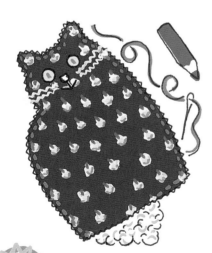

4 Stuff the cat with kapok. Use the end of a pencil to push the stuffing into the ears. Sew the gap closed.

5 Sew the strips of hessian together along 3 sides (2 long and one short). Stuff the tail through the open end. Fray the bottom of the tail. Sew the top end closed.

6 Sew the top of the tail to the side seam of the cat. Sew on a bow made with ribbon where the cat's neck would be.

FUN WITH FABRIC

ELEPHANT WALL HANGING

Make a beautifully decorated elephant with plenty of sequins and braid.

These sparkly leaf sequins are a good choice for finishing off the zigzag border.

you will need...

Wooden dowel, 1 cm (½ in) in diameter, about 50 cm (20 in) long

Orange, pale orange + blue felt, each about 30 cm (12 in) square

Pale blue felt, about 10 cm (4 in) square

Lilac felt, about 10 x 30 cm (4 x 12 in)

Braid ('ric-rac'), 1.5 m (1½ yd)

Ribbon, scraps

Sewing tape, 5 pieces each about 10 cm (4 in)

Blue paint + paintbrush

Sewing thread + needle

Assorted sequins + small beads

Paper string or cord, about 1 m (1 yd)

Scissors

Fabric glue

making the wall hanging...

1 From felt, cut an elephant (*blue*), an ear and a tusk (*pale blue*), and a saddle and headdress (*orange*).

2 Glue or sew the elephant onto the background panel of pale orange felt. Glue on the saddle, tusk and headdress.

3 Decorate the elephant, saddle and headdress with sequins, ribbon and braid, glued or sewn on. Decorate the ear and glue it in place.

4 Glue or sew on a large sequin for an eye. For the tail, thread sequins and beads alternately on thread, and sew onto the elephant.

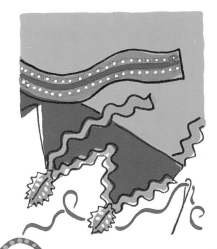

5 Cut a zigzag border in lilac felt to fit across the bottom of the wall hanging. Glue or sew it in place and glue ribbon over the join. Glue or sew braid to the sides and bottom of the wall hanging. Sew a sequin to each point of the zigzag.

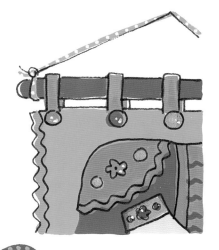

6 Sew tape loops to the top of the wall hanging, spacing them evenly. Sew a sequin on each. Paint the dowel blue and slide it through the loops. Tie string at each end of the dowel to hang the picture.

FUN WITH FABRIC

163

FELT BOOKMARKS

you will need...

For the Initials Bookmark

Assorted felt scraps, one at least
  7 x 25 cm (2³/₄ x 9 in)
Small bead or flat button
Paper
Pencil
Fabric glue
Pins
Needle
Sewing thread
Pinking
  shears
Scissors

Big, bold letters are easier to cut out and more striking.

Make a wiggly Snake with a 'ric-rac' tongue and beady eyes.

This racing car has button tyre trims and white felt puffs from its exhaust.

making a felt bookmark...

Initials

1 Draw the outline of your *bookmark*, your initials, the star and square on paper. Cut out these paper patterns.

2 Pin the paper patterns to felt scraps of different colours. Cut around the patterns to get the felt shapes you need.

3 Glue the felt letters to the felt book-mark. Glue the square in place, and glue the star over it.

4 Sew a bead or button in the centre of the star for decoration.

FUN WITH FABRIC

165

PYJAMA BAG

you will need...

Pillowcase

Fabric scraps, each at least
   10 x 15 cm (4 x 6 in)

Narrow ribbon or cord, about 1.5 m
   (1 1/2 yd)

Paper, a large sheet

Buttons

Pencil

Pins

Needle

Sewing thread

Safety pin

Scissors

Pinking shears

Fabric glue

Pull the loop at each side to close the bag.

Make the letters big and bold to fill the front of the pillowcase.

Use a star for the dot above the "i", and sew a button on to add a colourful touch.

making a pyjama bag...

1 Draw the letters for your name or your initials on paper. Draw a star for a dot. Cut out.

2 Pin each paper pattern to a scrap of fabric. Cut out the shapes with pinking shears.

3 Glue the fabric letters to the pillowcase. Make sure the opening of the pillowcase is at the top.

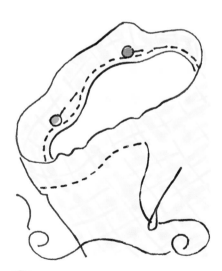

4 Sew around each letter using small running stitches, about 0.5 cm (1/4 in) from the edge (see page 247). Sew a button over any star dots you have used.

5 Pin a hem round the opening of the pillow-case, wide enough to take a ribbon. Sew the hem using running stitches, leaving a gap at each side seam.

6 Pin a safety pin to one end of the ribbon. Push through the gap into the hem, and thread the ribbon round the pillowcase twice. Sew the ribbon ends together.

RAINY DAY
fun with
beads + sequins

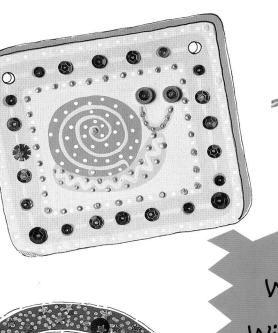

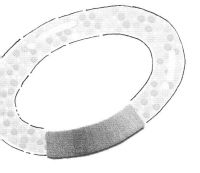

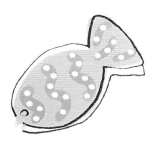

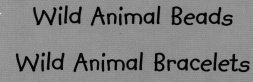

Wild Animal Beads

Wild Animal Bracelets

Glitter Necklace
+ Bracelets

Paper + Paper Clip
Pendant

Sequined Room Plaque

Jewellery Box

WILD ANIMAL BEADS

you will need...

Newspaper, torn into strips
Elastic or thread, about 60 cm (24 in)
Glue, diluted with water
Petroleum jelly
4 Knitting needles
Potato, cut in half
Paints
Paintbrushes
30 small wooden
    beads,
Varnish

Mix stripes and spots to make a really wild necklace, or stick to the markings of one animal and experiment with colour.

Alternate wild animal beads with small wooden beads.

making wild animal beads...

1 Mix the newspaper strips with glue to make papier mâché pulp (*see page 245*). Coat the knitting needles with petroleum jelly.

2 Take marble-sized lumps of papier mâché and mould them round a knitting needle to make small spheres. Leave a gap between each one. Repeat using the other knitting needles until you have enough beads.

3 Stick the knitting needles into the cut potato (don't let the beads touch). Leave them to dry for 5 days. Take the beads off the needles. Allow to dry for another day.

4 Paint the beads a plain colour. Allow to dry. Then paint on spots and stripes. Paint on a coat of varnish. Thread the beads onto elastic, alternating with wooden beads.

WILD ANIMAL BRACELETS

you will need...

Cardboard tube

Newspaper, torn into strips

Paints

Paintbrushes

Varnish

Glue, diluted with water

Scissors

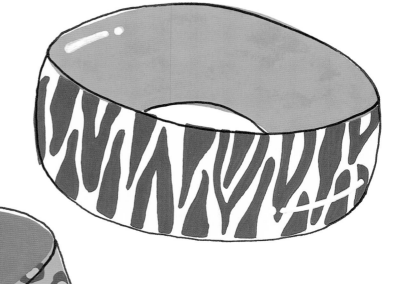

Clear, bold markings are the most eye-catching.

Paint the inside of the bracelets in a contrasting colour.

making a wild animal bracelet...

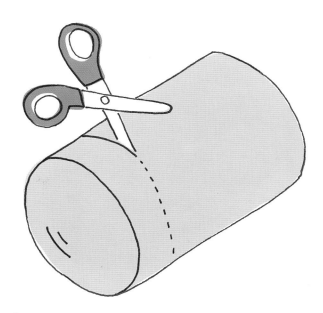

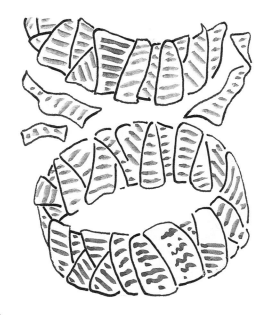

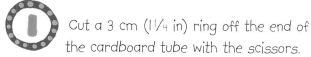 **1** Cut a 3 cm (1¼ in) ring off the end of the cardboard tube with the scissors.

2 Paste newspaper strips on the ring with dilute glue and a paintbrush. Cover the ring completely several times. Allow to dry.

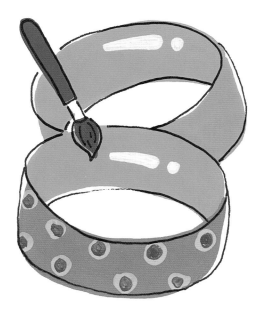

3 Paint the bracelet a base colour inside and out. Allow to dry.

4 Paint stripes or spots on the outside of the bracelet. Add a coat of varnish.

173

GLITTER NECKLACE + BRACELETS

you will need...

For the Fish Bracelet

Clear plastic tubing, about 20 cm (8 in)

Small lump of plastic or modelling putty

Coloured sand, from stores supplying
   aquariums

Balsa wood, about
   3 x 5 cm
   (1¼ x 2 in)

Glitter

Paints

Paintbrushes

Craft knife
   (be careful!)

Sticky tape

Embroidery
   thread

Jugs

Knitting needle

Glue

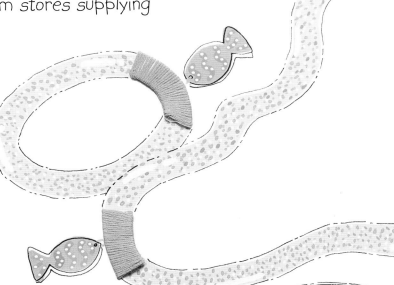

The necklace is made in the same way as the bracelet, only with a longer piece of tubing.

Fill the tubing with glitter, sequins, beads, seeds - even sherbet or tiny sweets!

You can bind the tubing with embroidery threads of different colours if you like.

making a glitter bracelet...

Fish

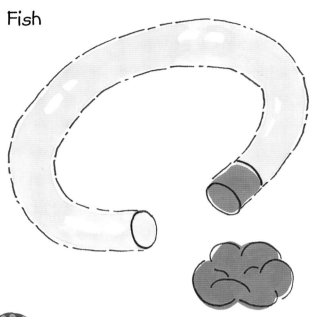

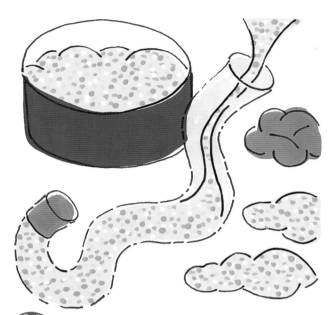

1 Cut a piece of tube to fit comfortably round your wrist. Plug one end of the tube with a small lump of putty.

2 Put the sand and glitter into a jug. Fill the tube. Plug the other end with putty.

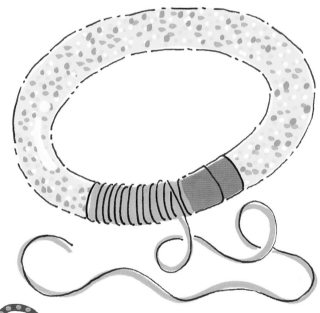

3 Tape the ends together. Bind the ends with embroidery thread to cover and strengthen the join. Glue as you go.

4 Cut a small fish out of balsa wood (copy the one above). Poke an eye hole with the knitting needle. Paint the fish on both sides. Hang the fish from the bangle with a piece of thread looped through the eye.

PAPER + PAPER CLIP PENDANT

you will need...

Assorted coloured paper, small sheets

3 or 4 plastic drinking straws

Chenille pipe cleaner, folded in half

Assorted beads, about 25

Embroidery thread or cord, about 1 m (1 yd)

Coloured paper clips, about 25

Scissors

Glue

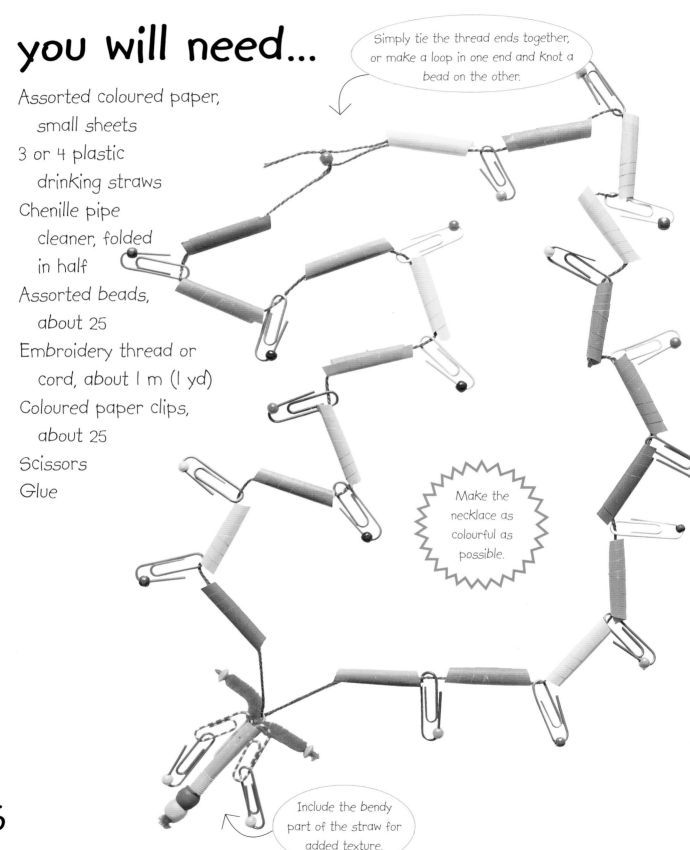

Simply tie the thread ends together, or make a loop in one end and knot a bead on the other.

Make the necklace as colourful as possible.

Include the bendy part of the straw for added texture.

making a paper clip pendant...

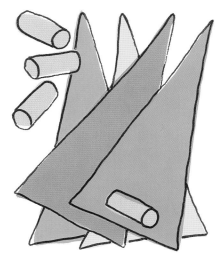

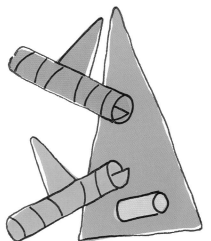

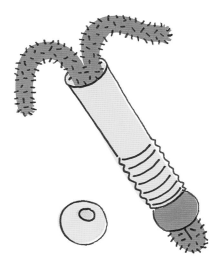

1 For paper *beads*, cut 20 tall (isosceles) paper triangles in different colours (trace the ones above). Cut the straws into 20 sections about 2-2.5 cm (¾-1 in) long.

2 Spread glue on the back of a triangle. Lay the straw on the *base* of the triangle and roll it up in the paper. Glue the tip of the triangle to hold it.

3 Push the folded pipe cleaner through a 4 cm (1½ in) piece of straw, cut just below the bend. Push 2 beads onto the fold.

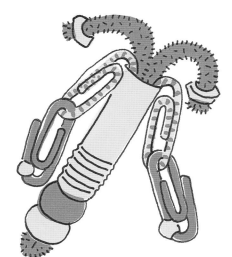

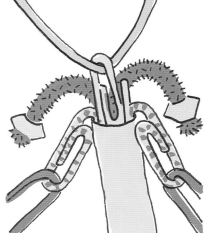

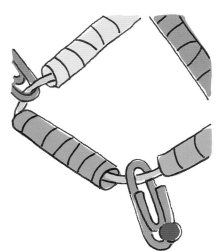

4 Push a *bead* onto each end of the pipe cleaner and bend the ends open. For each wing, hang 2 linked paper clips from the straw and thread a bead onto one.

5 Push a paper clip into the top of the straw as a hanging link. Glue the paper clips in place inside the straw.

6 Push a *bead* onto each remaining paper clip. Thread beads and paper clips alternately onto embroidery thread. Hang the pendant from the centre. Tie the ends.

FUN WITH BEADS + SEQUINS

177

SEQUINED ROOM PLAQUE

you will need...

For the Name Plaque

Salt dough (*see page 252*)

Paints + paintbrushes

Sequins, tiny beads

Varnish

Rolling pin

Knife

Ruler

Baking tray

Metal skewer

Coloured cord or
   embroidery thread
   about 30 cm
   (12 in)

The Snail has beads glued all over his body and shell, and his feelers are beads with sequins glued on top.

Paint the plaque in pastel colours, then paint the name and add hearts and patterns in bold, contrasting colours.

Glue tiny beads to the letters of the name, and decorate the border with sequins.

making a room plaque...

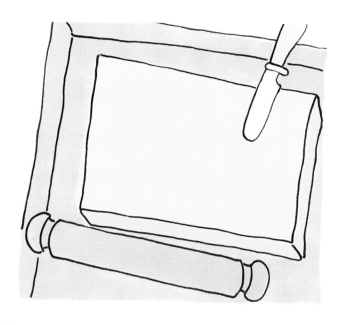

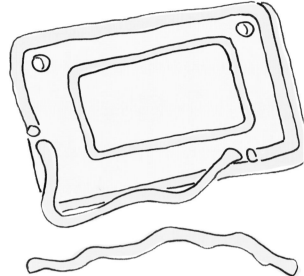

1 Roll out the salt dough. Measure out a piece 21 × 30 cm (8¼ × 12 in) using the ruler. Cut it out and place it on a baking tray (see page 252).

2 Roll out long thin sausages of dough. Use these to make an inner and outer border for the plaque. Join short pieces in place. Make a hole in the top 2 corners with the skewer.

3 Roll out more thin sausages to make the letters and the border. Bake the plaque (see page 252). Allow to dry.

4 Paint the plaque. Paint on a coat of varnish. Glue on beads and sequins. Hang the plaque from cord tied at the holes.

JEWELLERY BOX

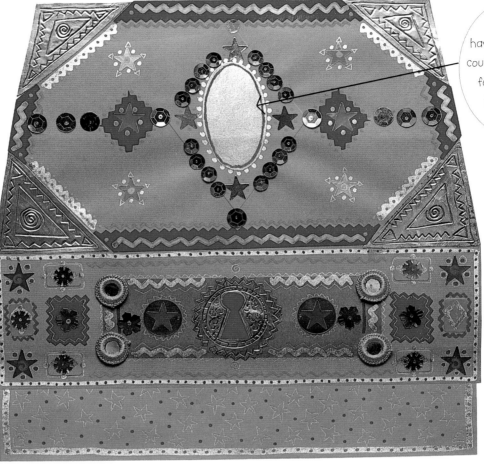

Use lots of sequins, sparkly stars and coloured paper shapes, embellished with silver pen, to lavishly decorate the box.

If you don't have a mirror, you could use an oval of foil to decorate the centre of the lid.

you will need...

Cardboard box, shoe box-sized
Purple and blue paint + paintbrushes
Small oval mirror
Dark blue, mid blue + green paper, small sheets
Thick silver foil
Dry ballpoint pen

Stickers, sequins
Felt tip pens, silver marker pen
Embroidery thread in 3 colours or ribbon, about 60 cm (24 in)
Old Key
Scissors, pinking shears
Glue

making a jewellery box...

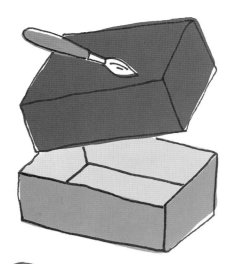

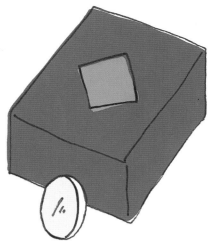

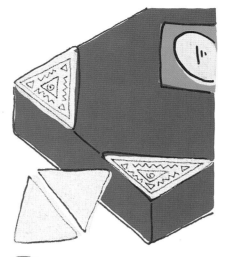

1 Paint the outside of the bottom of the box blue, and the lid purple.

2 Cut a diamond from mid blue paper. Glue it in the centre of the box lid. Glue the mirror in the centre of the diamond.

3 Cut two 6 cm ($2^3/_8$ in) squares of foil in half to make 4 triangles. Draw patterns on the triangles with the ballpoint pen. Glue triangles to the corners of the lid.

4 Glue a strip of green paper to one long side of the lid. Glue on a foil circle, cut with pinking shears and decorated. Glue on a dark blue paper keyhole.

5 Decorate the lid with sequins, stickers, felt pens and silver pen. Draw a pattern on the bottom of the box with felt pens and silver pen.

6 Twist together the 3 colours of embroidery thread to make a cord. Loop the cord through the key and knot the end.

FUN WITH BEADS + SEQUINS

181

MAKE-BELIEVE
dressing up

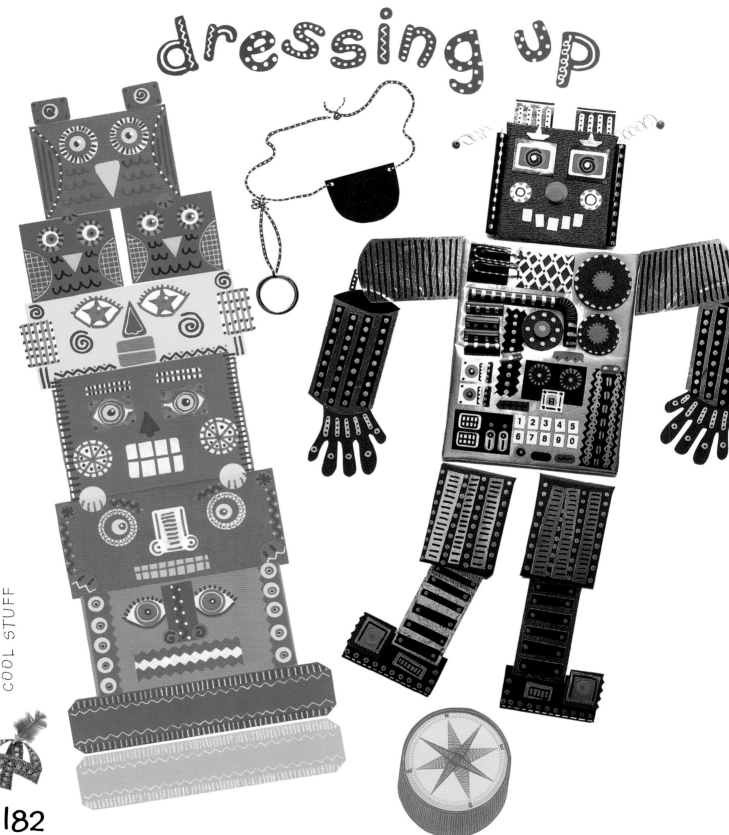

Explorer

Pirate

Native American

Knight

Astronaut

EXPLORER rainforest

you will need...

Green, blue + yellow paper or
   paper card, large sheets
Thin card in bright colours,
   small sheets
Pipe cleaners, coloured
Washing line or string/twine, hung
   between 2 poles or trees
Plastic garden netting
Paints
Paintbrushes
Sponge
Pencil
Felt tip pens
Stickers
Clothes pegs or paper clips
Scissors
Pinking shears
Glue

making a rainforest...

① Sponge yellow, green and blue paint onto the sheets of paper to make different patterns and textures.

② Draw leaf shapes on the painted paper with a pencil. Cut out the leaves.

Butterfly

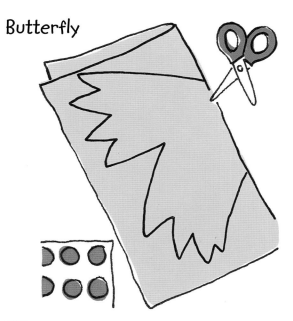

③ Decide on the animals that will inhabit your rainforest. You may want to add to my collection of birds, butterflies, frogs and snakes.

④ Fold a sheet of yellow card in half. Draw half a butterfly on one side. Cut out. You will have a pair of wings joined in the middle.

and the animals...

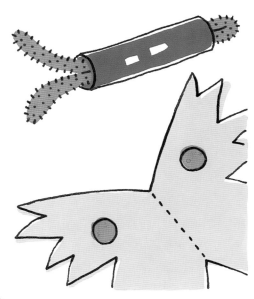

Bird

5 Fold a pipe cleaner in half and push the fold down a 3 cm (1 ¼ in) piece of straw. Decorate the wings with stickers.

6 Cut a bird body and wing from *blue* card. Paint a beak, an eye and feather details on the body, and feathers on the wing.

Lemur

7 Cut the lemur and tail from brown card. Add sticker eyes. Draw in a nose and mouth and add arm and leg details with felt pen.

8 Hang the netting over the washing line. Peg or clip the foliage, flowers and forest creatures to the netting. Clip some foliage to the back of the netting too, for added depth.

EXPLORER compass + binoculars

you will need...

For the Compass

Coffee jar lid

Red + green coloured paper,
   small sheets

Felt tip pens

Crayons

Scissors

Paper fastener

Darning needle

Glue

The zigzag pattern makes the pointers look as if they are trembling, just as real compass needles do.

Gently move the pointers so that they point to differe points of the compass.

For the Binoculars

2 small cardboard tubes

2 larger cardboard tubes,
   paper towel inner, cut in half

Paints + paintbrushes

Coloured paper, small sheets

Egg carton

Bottle top

Ribbon or tape, about 70 cm (27½ in)

Double-sided tape

Sticky tape

Stapler

Scissors

Glue

Paint or draw focus controls in black and white.

Loop the ribbon over a strap of coloured paper and staple onto the tube for a realistic look.

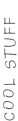

making the compass + binoculars...

Compass

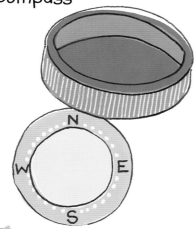
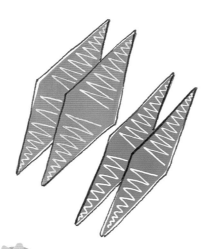
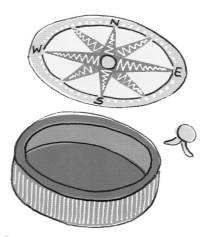

1 Remove card from lid. Colour the card yellow with crayon. Divide the circle into quarters. Use a felt tip to mark in N (North), S (South), E (East) and W (West).

2 Cut 2 large diamond-shaped pointers from red paper and 2 smaller pointers from green. Draw a zigzag pattern on each pointer with felt pen.

3 With the needle, make a small hole through the centre of each pointer and the card. Push a paper fastener through the green pointers, then the red, and then the card. Glue back into the lid.

Binoculars

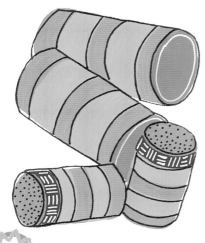

1 Paint the inside of the larger tubes blue or grey to look like lenses. Glue strips of paper around all 4 tubes to make stripes. Paint black and white focus controls.

2 Cut 2 rings from the egg carton. Glue them to the openings of the small tubes. Paint the rings black. Stick the bottle top between the small tubes with double-sided tape or glue.

3 Stick the large tubes onto the small tubes with double-sided tape. Staple each end of the ribbon strap to a large tube.

PIRATE hat, beard, eye patch + earring

you will need...

Give the skull a ghoulish grin with black felt pen.

For the Pirate Hat

Thick black paper, about
    45 x 60 cm (18 x 24 in)

White paper, about
    25 x 50 cm (10 x 20 in)

Black felt tip pen

Stapler

Scissors

Glue

If you have no black paper, cut the hat out of white paper, trace on the skull and crossbones and paint black all except the skull and crossbones.

Loop the elastic round your ears to hold the beard in place.

For the Beard

Thick black paper, about 30 cm
    (12 in) square

Black wool or raffia or thread

Shirring elastic, about
    75 cm (30 in)

Hole punch

Scissors

Glue

Trim the wool around the edges of the beard shape and keep the mouth opening clear.

For the Eye Patch + Earring

Thick black paper, about 10 cm (4 in)
    square

Shirring elastic, about 75 cm (30 in)

Curtain ring

Scissors

The eye patch elastic goes over one ear and under the other to hold the patch in place.

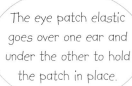

making a hat, beard, eye patch + earring...

Hat

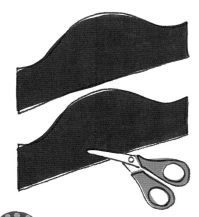

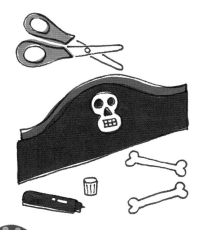

1 Fold the black paper in half and cut out 2 hat shapes with the scissors. Copy the shape of the hat (*see opposite page*).

2 Cut out a skull and crossbones from white paper. Glue onto the front of the hat. Add skull features in pen. Staple the 2 hat pieces together at the sides, to fit your head.

Beard

1 Cut out a beard shape from the *black paper*. Cut a smile shape for a mouth. Punch a hole on each side of the beard with the hole punch.

2 Glue on enough wool to cover the paper beard. Trim around the edges and the mouth. Tie a piece of elastic at each side, and make 2 loops at the ends, to go around your ears.

Eye patch + Earring

1 Cut out an eye patch from *black paper*. Make a small hole at each side and thread elastic through. Tie at the back to fit your head.

2 Tie a piece of elastic to the curtain ring. Make a loop and tie onto the eye patch elastic, so that when you are wearing the eye patch, the earring hangs down next to your ear.

DRESSING UP

191

PIRATE treasure chest

you will need...

Cardboard box, shoe box-sized

Brown paint + paintbrush

Black paper, a large sheet

Metallic crayon, bronze

Paper fasteners

Gold or yellow round stickers

Card discs of
   different
   coin sizes

Silver + gold
   foil

Dry ballpoint pen

Black felt tip pen

Paper clips

Bradawl or
   darning
   needle

Scissors

Glue

Fill your chest with gold doubloons, pieces of eight and precious chains you have made, as well as costume jewellery and any other sparkly treasures.

Once you have a chest full of priceless treasure, perhaps you should think about a really secret hiding place - and a treasure map!

The markings on the coins are made by drawing on the foil with a dry ballpoint pen.

making a treasure chest...

1 Paint the box and lid brown to look like wood. Allow to dry.

2 Rub the crayon on the black paper to make it shine. Cut the paper into strips about 3-4 cm (1-1½ in) wide. Glue the strips onto the box to make stripes.

3 Use the bradawl to make holes in the stripes. To make studs, push a paper fastener through each hole and open out on the inside of the box.

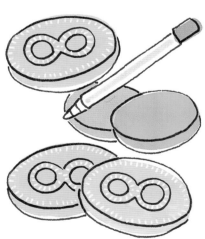

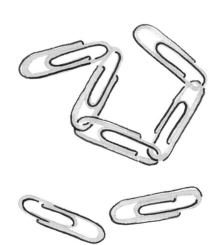

4 Draw a keyhole shape (trace the one above) on a gold/yellow sticker in black felt tip pen. Stick on the front of the box.

5 Wrap card discs in foil or cover on both sides with a gold/yellow sticker. Draw on coin markings with a dry ballpoint pen, or draw on the stickers with felt pen.

6 Link together paper clips to make chains of different lengths for necklaces and bracelets.

NATIVE AMERICAN
plaited headband + neck purse

you will need...

For the Headband

Black raffia or wool, cut into 25 cm
  (10 in) lengths
4 coloured feathers
Broad ribbon, about 45 cm (18 in)
Braid, about 45 cm (18 in)
Elastic, about 10 cm (4 in)
Assorted coloured beads
Embroidery thread, in one or
  2 bright colours
Embroidery needle
Sewing thread
Needle
Scissors
Glue

Hook the tied end of the raffia bunches onto a doorknob or coat hook to hold it still while you plait the raffia.

Sew or glue beads on singly, or sew a string of beads onto the headband.

Catch in a feather or tie on a few beads at the end of the plait.

This purse has a fringe made of strips of ribbon, caught into the bottom seam of the purse.

Bury the end of the embroidery thread by pushing it back into the tightly-wound thread, using the needle.

For the Neck Purse

Felt or fabric, 2 pieces each about
  12 x 16 cm (5 x 6½ in)
Shoelace or narrow ribbon, about
  45 cm (18 in)
Narrow ribbon, a scrap
2 coloured feathers

Assorted coloured beads
Sewing thread, embroidery thread
Needle, embroidery needle
Scissors
Pinking shears
Glue

making a headband + purse...

Headband

1 Wind sewing thread around the top ends of 2 bunches of raffia. Plait the raffia. Wind embroidery thread round the bottom ends.

2 Glue braid onto the broad ribbon. Sew elastic onto each end of the ribbon to make a circle which fits round your head.

3 Sew or glue beads onto the headband for decoration. Sew a plait to each side. Finish with 2 feathers, sewn or glued on at the back.

Purse

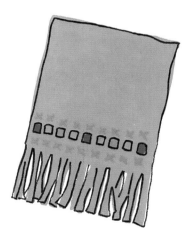

1 Fold down one piece of felt 4 cm (1½ in) from the top. Cut the fold into an envelope flap shape. This is the back of the purse.

2 Cut a 4 cm (1½ in) fringe on the bottom of the other piece of felt (the front of the purse). Glue or sew on beads and work a row of cross-stitch on either side.

3 Sew the felt pieces on 3 sides. Sew a bead on the front and a ribbon loop on the flap. Knot beads and sew feathers on the shoe lace before sewing it to the purse.

195

NATIVE AMERICAN totem pole

you will need...

2 old tyres
Cardboard boxes of different sizes
Lids, tubes, egg boxes
Acrylic paints in bright colours
Poster paints in bright colours
Paintbrushes
Parcel tape
Stickers
Glue

Owl faces like these are a good example of what can be done with paint, felt pen and stickers.

The uglier the face and the fiercer the expression, the better!

Don't forget to decorate your totem pole on all sides.

Practise your most energetic 'rain dance' around a totem pole like this one.

making a totem pole...

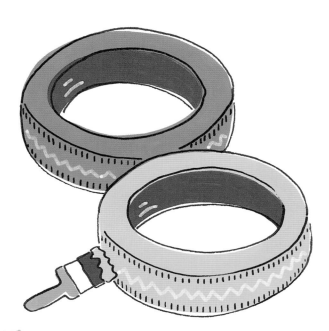

1 Paint the tyres with acrylic paints. Put one on top of the other. (You may need help with this.)

2 Tape the boxes shut. Paint the boxes in a variety of poster paint colours.

3 Paint funny faces, monster faces and designs on the boxes. Tape or glue on lids, egg cartons and tubes and paint them too, for a 3-D effect. Use stickers for added detail.

4 Tape the boxes together one on top of the other, and paint over the tape. Push the bottom box into the tyres to stop the totem pole from falling over.

197

KNIGHT helmet + tunic

you will need...

For the Helmet

Thick black paper, a large sheet

Metallic crayon, silver

Plastic wall plug

Feathers

Stapler

Paper
   fasteners

Glue

Silver or gold stickers would make bright studs too, or draw them in with marker pen.

If you have no wall plugs, bind the feathers with colour thread and glue on the helmet.

For the Tunic

Fabric or strong paper, 2 pieces each
   about 30 x 50 cm (12 x 20 in)

Fabric in contrasting colour,
   about 40 x 60 cm (16 x 24 in)

Fabric tape or bias binding,
   about 80 cm (31½ in)

Stapler

Sewing thread

Needle

Scissors

Glue or fusible web

Draw in the bird's eye details with felt pen.

The bird could also be traced straight onto the tunic and then painted with fabric paint.

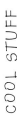

making a helmet + tunic...

Helmet

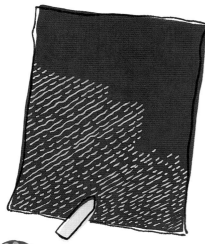

1 Rub the crayon over the black paper to give it a shiny metallic look.

2 Cut a strip of paper 4 × 60 cm (1½ × 24 in). Staple it to fit your head. Cut 2 strips about 4 × 34 cm (1½ × 13½ in). Staple these on side to side and front to back.

3 Cut a noseguard from the paper. Attach it to the helmet with a paper fastener. Decorate the helmet with paper fastener studs.

Tunic

4 Glue feathers into the wall plug. Glue the plug to the top of the helmet.

1 Cut the fabric tape into 4 equal lengths. Staple, sew or glue on 2 pieces as shoulder straps (leave a gap for your head), and the other 2 across the sides.

2 Fold the contrasting fabric in half. Cut 2 bird shapes. Stick one on the front and one on the back of the tunic with glue or fusible web (see page 248).

199

KNIGHT'S shield

you will need...

Large cardboard box, flattened

Thin card, about 4 x 15 cm
   (1¹/₂ x 6 in)

Paints + paintbrushes

Pencil

Felt tip pens

Parcel tape or sticky tape

Scissors

Copy this castle design for a simple but striking decoration.

The fleur de lys is a simplified lily, and was a popular heraldic emblem.

The owl, like the falcon and eagle, were symbols of power and bravery.

Use colourful paint, felt tip pen and stickers to decorate your shield.

making a shield...

Fleur de lys

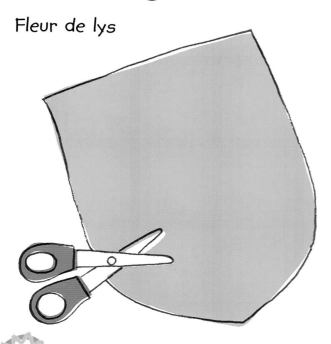

1 Cut the shield shape from the cardboard.

2 Draw the fleur de lys design in pencil on the shield.

3 Paint the fleur de lys and the background. Use felt tip pen to add detail.

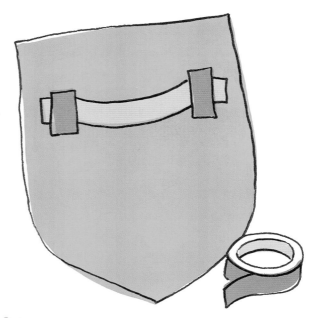

4 To make a handle, tape the card to the back of the shield. Make sure the handle is big enough for you to grasp.

DRESSING UP

201

ASTRONAUT jetpack

The radio is a matchbox painted black and decorated with silver marker pen, stickers and a coiled-wire antenna.

Use your imagination and invent gadgets and gizmos galore. Your jetpack can be whatever colour you choose.

The plastic bottles are stuck upside down.

The control panel can be made from cardboard or paper.

you will need...

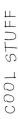

Large cereal box

Grey + black paint + paintbrushes

2 plastic bottles with tops

Paper or thin card, about
    15 cm (6 in) square

Assorted lids (small jars, bottles)

Polystyrene or frozen pizza backing,
    about 10 x 25 cm (4 x 10 in)

Matchbox

202 Black + silver marker pens

Silver, black, white, number stickers

Scrap of coiled, thin wire

Small bead

Fabric or webbing, 2 strips each
    about 5 x 50 cm (2 x 20 in)

Silver foil

Parcel tape or sticky tape

Scissors

Glue

making a jetpack...

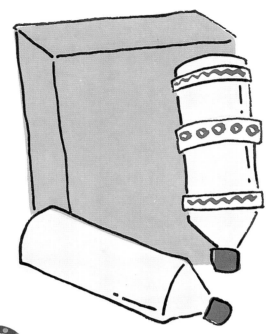

1 Tape the lid of the cereal box shut. Paint the box grey.

2 Cover the bottles with silver foil. Glue the bottles onto the box, with tops facing down. Cut 6 strips of paper about 2 x 15 cm (³/₄ x 6 in). Decorate using stickers or silver and black marker pens. Glue a strap over the top, middle and bottom of each bottle.

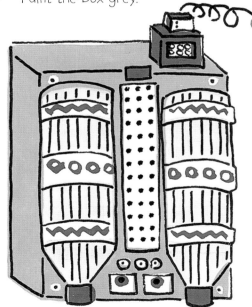

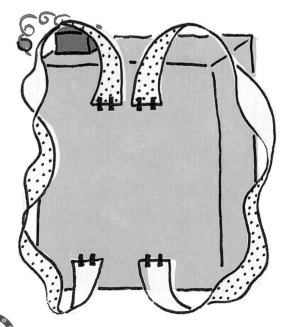

3 Thread the bead onto the wire. Tape the wire to the matchbox. Glue the matchbox to the top of the box. Paint the matchbox black. Glue a strip of polystyrene between the bottles. Add dials and control buttons with stickers, marker pen, and glued-on painted lids.

4 Tape or glue the fabric strips onto the box so you can wear it like a backpack.

DRESSING UP

ASTRONAUT robot

you will need...

Assorted cardboard boxes,
Assorted cardboard tubes
Assorted lids
Paint, black, silver, red
Paintbrushes
Old rubber gloves
2 plastic bottles (squash
   or bubble bath)
Foam scrap, cut into a
   small circle
Silver foil
2 scraps of thin wire,
   coiled
2 beads
White, black, silver + numbered
   stickers
Silver marker pen
Black marker pen
Paper clips
Parcel tape or sticky tape
Elastic, about 1.5 m (1½ yd)
Scissors
Glue

Paint the foam nose red before gluing to the Robot's face.

Make Robot shiny with silver stickers and silver marking pen.

The elastic threaded through the arms gives them movement.

Use lids, tubes, stickers – and your imagination – to make buttons, levers and flashing lights.

Try to match up the size of boxes and tubes on either side.

COOL STUFF

making a robot...

1 First, sort out the boxes and tubes you will need. Head: a medium-sized box. Arm: a tube and a bottle. Leg: a shoe box (foot), a medium-sized box (calf) and a larger box (thigh).

2 Paint the glove hands black and silver. Cover 2 tubes and 2 bottles with foil. Tie elastic round the wrist of a glove and thread it through a tube and a bottle. Do the same for the other arm.

3 Cover a large box with silver foil. Cut a round hole in each side for the arms to fit tightly into. Tie the elastic from the 2 arms together inside the box. Then tape the box shut.

4 For control buttons, glue lids onto the body. Stick on stickers, silver foil, tubes and paper clips and add details with a marker pen.

5 Cut a hole in the lid of the shoe box for the leg to fit tightly into. Tape the 3 leg boxes together before painting black and silver. Tape the thigh boxes to the body.

6 Paint the head box black. Stick on a foam nose and stickers for eyes and mouth. Add a bead to each wire, tape to the matchboxes. Glue to the head and attach the body.

MAKE-BELIEVE
my second home

Hide

Pirate Ship

Tepee

Castle

Space Rocket

207

HIDE

you will need...

8 bamboo canes, 4 long, 4 shorter

Large piece of fabric, the size of a
   double sheet

Green, yellow or blue
   scraps of crepe
   paper, fabric, felt
   + card

Paints

Paintbrushes

String or twine,
   about 2 m (2 yd)

Pencil

Safety pins

Clothes pegs

Pinking shears

Scissors

Take cover in your hide and watch the exotic birds and animals of the rainforest in secret.

If you have permission, glue the leaves onto the fabric so that you can use your hide again and again.

Choose fabric in a dark colour to blend in with the forest.

Try and cover the fabric with leaves of different shapes, colours and textures.

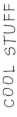

making a hide...

1 Push the 4 long canes into the ground to make a square frame. Tie the shorter canes around the top with string.

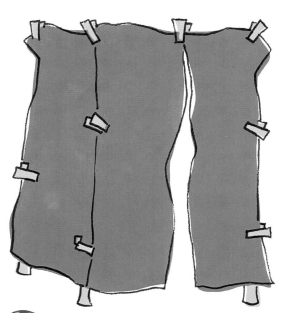

2 Lay the fabric over the frame and peg it onto the canes to hold it in place. Let the edges of the fabric just overlap at the front, to make an entrance.

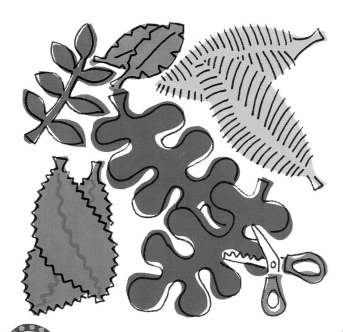

3 Cut leaves from crepe paper, felt and card with scissors. Cut fabric leaves with pinking shears. Paint some of the paper and card leaves.

4 Pin the leaves all over the hide with safety pins. Close the entrance with a safety pin or clothes peg, leaving a gap big enough for your binoculars to fit through.

MY SECOND HOME

PIRATE SHIP

you will need...

3 cardboard boxes, 2 medium + one large

Paints + paintbrushes

2 plastic or cardboard tubes

Ping pong balls

Small doll

Black fabric or card, about
   10 x 20 cm (4 x 8 in)

White fabric or paper, about
   10 x 20 cm (4 x 8 in)

3 garden canes

Broom, or just the
   handle

2 pillowcases

Cardboard, about
   10 cm (4 in) square

Ball of string

Hole punch

Craft Knife (be careful!)

Darning needle

Clothes pegs

Stapler

Scissors

Glue

Use paint or felt tip pens to add detail to the ship, the flag, and even, if you have permission, to the pillowcase sails.

If you make flags from black card, glue them to the cane and the mast instead of tying them.

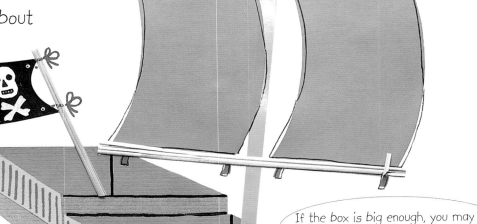

If the box is big enough, you may able to go aboard your pirate shi[p]

Paint cardboard cannons grey on the inside.

Weigh anch[or] by pulling on string insi[de] the ship.

making a pirate ship...

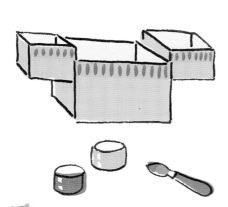

1 Staple the 2 smaller boxes to each end of the large box so that they sit slightly higher than the large box. Paint the ship on all sides.

2 Paint the tubes black. With the craft knife, cut 2 holes in the large box just big enough for the cannons to squeeze through. Paint balls black for cannonballs.

3 Cut an anchor from cardboard and paint black. Punch a hole at the top, tie the string through it. Push the end into a hole in the box and tape down.

4 Make 2 holes in the bow (front) of the ship with the needle. Loop the string round the doll, push the string through the holes and tie the ends together inside the box.

5 Make 2 Jolly Rogers. Punch 2 holes in each. Tie one to a cane with string, and tape to the stern (back) of the ship.

6 Bind 2 canes across the broom handle with string. Peg the pillowcase sails to each side of the mast. Tie the second flag to the top of the mast with string.

211

TEPEE
you will need...

3 long bamboo canes

String or twine, about 1 m (1 yd)

Large piece of fabric,
    such as an old sheet

Fabric paints + paintbrushes

42 ribbon or fabric tape strips,
    each about 15 cm (6 in) long

Pencil

Sewing thread

Needle

Pinking shears

Tie colourful ribbon or tape to the top of the tepee as decoration.

Cut the fabric with pinking shears to prevent it from fraying.

Dress up in your beaded headband and neck purse and invite your friends to a real pow-wow in your tepee.

The tepee is not waterproof, so don't forget to bring it indoors if it rains!

COOL STUFF

making a tepee...

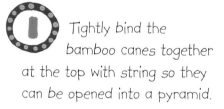
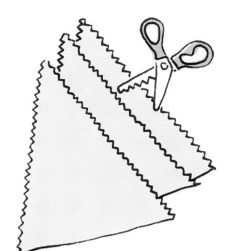

1 Tightly bind the bamboo canes together at the top with string so they can be opened into a pyramid.

2 Cut 3 identical triangles of fabric with sides the same length as the canes.

3 Cut a slit in one triangle from the centre of the bottom edge to half way up the triangle for the opening flap.

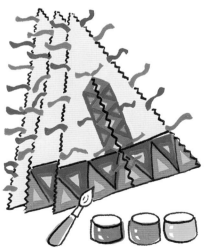

4 Sew a ribbon tie to the top, middle and bottom of each side of the flap (6 in all). Sew 6 ties evenly-spaced on the sides of the 3 triangles (36 in all).

5 Draw a border design in pencil along the bottom of each triangle and the opening flap of the tepee. Paint the border design in bright colours.

6 Push the canes into the ground to make a pyramid shape (you may need help with this). Tie the fabric onto the bamboo frame with the ribbon ties.

213

CASTLE

you will need...

Large cardboard box
4 cardboard tubes, from paper towel
Cardboard, about 15 cm (6 in) square
Card, about 20 x 30 cm (8 x 12 in)
Paints + paintbrushes
4 thin garden canes (no sharp points)
Twine or string, about 40 cm (16 in)

Felt tip pens
Craft Knife (be careful!)
Double-sided tape (optional)
Darning needle
Scissors
Glue

Place the castle on a piece of blue fabric just bigger than the box – and lower the drawbridge over the moat you have made!

Cut flags from coloured paper card and add bright stickers for your own design.

Outline the battlements with felt tip pen.

Raise and lower the drawbridge from within the castle by pulling or releasing the twine.

Paint the door blue before adding a black portcullis drawn in felt pen.

making a castle...

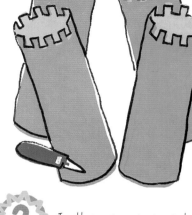

1 With the craft knife, cut notches all round the top of the box. (An adult should help you with this.) Space the notches evenly.

2 In the same way, cut evenly-spaced notches around the top of the 4 cardboard tubes.

3 Glue the tubes to the box (or use double-sided tape), 2 at the front and 2 at the back.

4 Paint the castle in the following colours: red archery slits, blue windows, a red arch over a blue door and a black portcullis.

5 Cut the cardboard to cover the arch. Fold the bottom 1 cm (½ in) and glue under the box. Push the needle threaded with twine through the drawbridge and arch and back through the drawbridge. Knot the ends of the twine.

6 Draw and paint 4 flags with a design of your choice on the card. Glue each one onto a cane. Tape one cane to the inside of each tower.

215

SPACE ROCKET

you will need...

Large grey or white cardboard box, big enough to sit in

2 cardboard tubes

Thin card, about 50 cm (20 in) square

Corrugated cardboard, about 8 × 30 cm (3¼ × 12 in)

Yellow, red, orange coloured tissue or cellophane

Paints

Paintbrushes

Stickers

Felt tip pens

Parcel tape

Sticky tape

String

Darning needle

Scissors

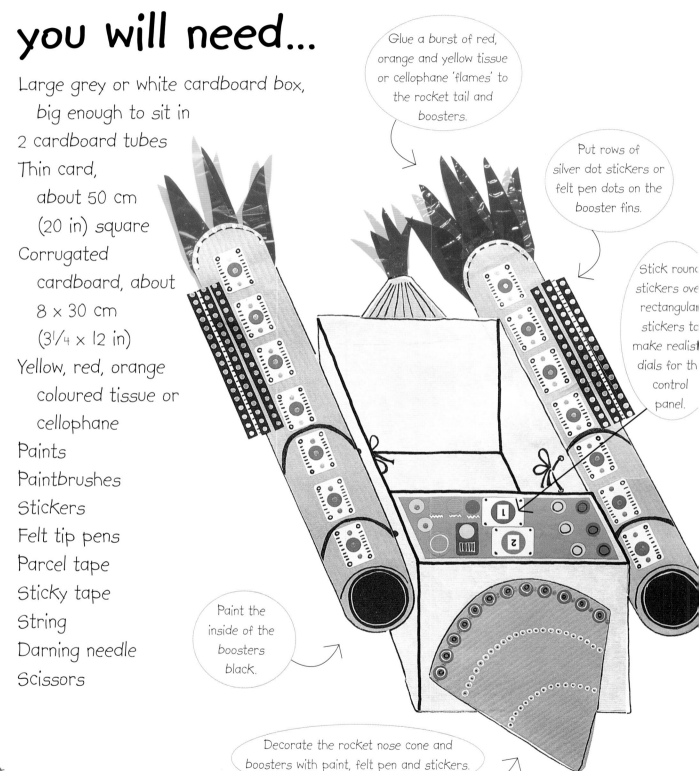

Glue a burst of red, orange and yellow tissue or cellophane 'flames' to the rocket tail and boosters.

Put rows of silver dot stickers or felt pen dots on the booster fins.

Stick round stickers over rectangular stickers to make realistic dials for the control panel.

Paint the inside of the boosters black.

Decorate the rocket nose cone and boosters with paint, felt pen and stickers.

making a space rocket...

1. Cut 3 flaps off the box, leaving the front flap for the control panel. Use stickers and felt pens to make buttons and dials on the control panel.

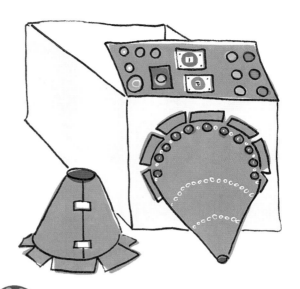

2. Cut one small and one large semicircle from card. Tape each into a cone. Cut the point off the small cone. Cut notches around the bottom of the cones and fold back. Tape the large cone to the front, and the small cone to the back. Paint the tape to match the box.

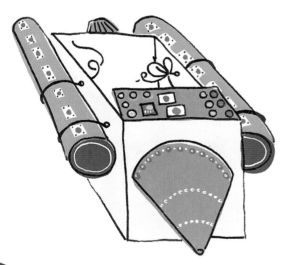

3. Paint the tubes to look like boosters. Loop string around the front of each tube, thread through 2 holes in the side of the box, and tie on the inside. Make another loop for the back of each tube.

4. Paint the corrugated card side fins. Glue a fin onto each booster. Tape or glue strips of tissue or cellophane into the boosters and tail of the rocket to look like flames.

217

MAKE-BELIEVE
Puppets

Wiggly Snake
Puppets

Life-size Concertina
Puppets

Finger Puppets

Wooden Spoon
Puppets

Sock Puppets

PUPPETS

WIGGLY SNAKE puppets

you will need...

For the Tube Snake

Cardboard tubes

Coloured paper, a scrap

Paint + paintbrushes

Stickers

String or wool, about 1 m (1 yd)

2 short sticks or plant canes
(no sharp points)

2 beads

Darning needle

Scissors

Glue

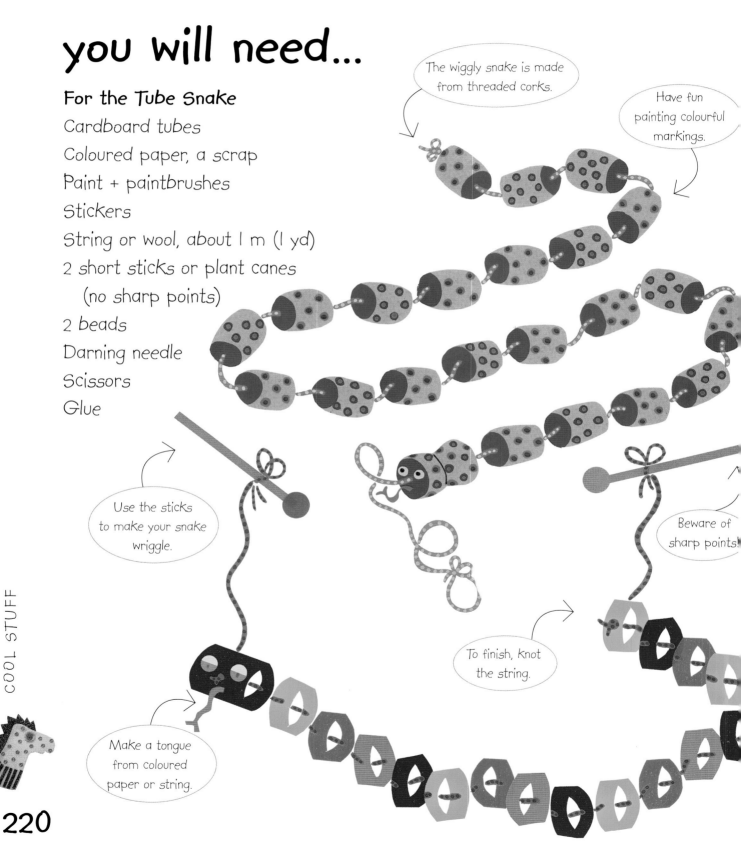

The wiggly snake is made from threaded corks.

Have fun painting colourful markings.

Use the sticks to make your snake wriggle.

Beware of sharp points!

To finish, knot the string.

Make a tongue from coloured paper or string.

making a wiggly puppet...

Tube Snake

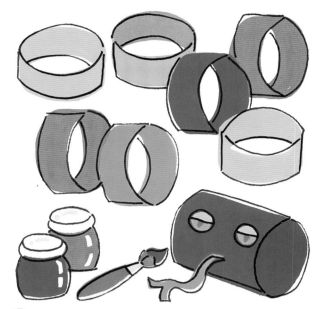

1 Cut up the tubes into rings about 3 cm (1¼ in) long to make the body of the snake. Cut a longer tube for the head.

2 Paint and decorate the tubes inside and out. On the head tube, paint eyes (or use stickers) and glue on a string/paper tongue.

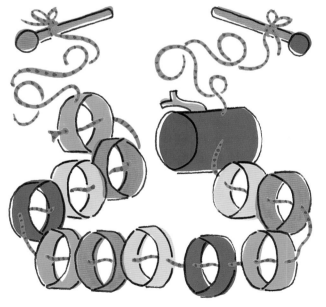

3 Thread the rings onto the string. Using the needle, push the string through the cardboard of the head and tail tubes. Knot the string to keep it there.

4 Glue a bead to one end of each stick. Tie a piece of string to each stick, then tie one string to the head and one string to the tail.

LIFE-SIZE CONCERTINA puppets

you will need...

Thin card, about 75 × 70 cm (30 × 27½ in) for face,
   body, arms and legs

Cardboard, about
   36 × 8 cm
   (14 × 3 in)
   for shoulders

Coloured paper

Paints

Paintbrushes

Stickers

String or wool

Wool or raffia

Sticky tape

Felt tip pens

Scissors

Glue or
   stapler

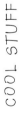

222

Cut a nose from thin card and glue onto face.

Draw in freckles with felt pen.

Use stickers to add detail and colour.

Glue paper to card for this skirt.

Push wool or string laces through a small hole in the card and then tie in a bow.

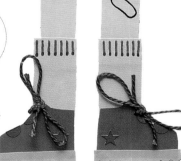

making a concertina puppet...

1 On a 20 x 60 cm (8 x 24 in) piece of card, paint a jumper and shorts or skirt. Fold the card concertina-style every 5 cm (2 in) down its length.

2 From card, cut out arms with hands (trace round your own) and legs with shoes. Paint and decorate the sleeves, socks and shoes with stickers and felt pen.

3 Cut out a head the same width (20 cm/ 8 in) as the body. Draw on a mouth and use stickers for eyes and cheeks. Glue on paper and wool or raffia for hair.

4 Glue or staple the legs to the body. Then stick or staple the head, arms and body onto the shoulders. To carry your puppet, tape a loop of string to the back of head.

FINGER puppets
you will need...

For the Leopard Puppet

Orange felt, about 15 cm (6 in) square

Yellow felt, about 7 x 5 cm
   (2³/₄ x 2 in)

Black felt, a scrap

2 small buttons

Felt tip pen

Yellow + orange
   spot stickers

Pipe cleaners or
   straw

Black + yellow sewing
   thread

Needle

Pinking shears

Glue

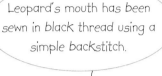
Use the yellow and orange stickers to make Leopard's spots.

Leopard's mouth has been sewn in black thread using a simple backstitch.

Ladybird's antennae are beads threaded on plastic loops.

Panda has a black and white felt head and a scrap of ribbon just for fun.

Make a crazy Owl with scraps of braid, stickers and a sewn-on paper clip.

making a finger puppet...

Leopard

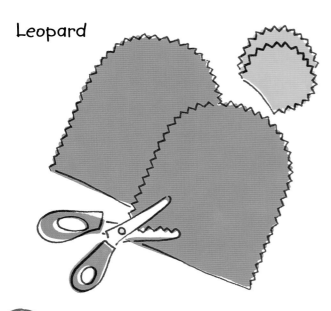

1 Fold your orange felt in half using pinking shears, cut 2 pieces of for the puppet, and 2 small yellow felt ears.

2 For the face, sew button eyes onto one piece of orange felt, glue on a black felt nose and sew (or draw in with felt pen) a black mouth (see page 247).

3 Put the ears at the top of the head between the 2 pieces of orange felt. Sew the 2 pieces of orange felt together using yellow thread and a running stitch (see page 247).

4 Make leopard spots with stickers or felt pen. Make a tiny slit either side of Leopard's face and thread through pipe cleaners or straw for the whiskers.

WOODEN SPOON puppets

Goldilocks has wool hair glued in place, then plaited and tied with ribbon.

A string, raffia and wool mane for Leonardo.

Tie on a fabric dress with a bright wool bow.

Stiff card ears and a fabric bowtie for Bunny.

Glue fabric on a pointy cardboard hat and glue it over the hair.

you will need...

For Leonardo
Wooden spoon

2 small buttons

Paints + paintbrushes

Felt tip pens

Orange + yellow paper

Yellow + brown wool scraps

226 String + raffia scraps

Garden twine makes wonderful Witch's hair.

Yellow + brown felt scraps

Glue

Scissors

making a spoon puppet...

Leonardo

1 Glue button eyes and a brown felt nose in the hollow of the spoon. Draw in a mouth with felt pen.

2 Cut a zigzag mane from orange paper and glue it to the back of the spoon. Cut ears from yellow paper and glue on.

3 Stick small scraps of yellow and brown wool, raffia and string to the orange mane.

4 Glue on yellow felt whiskers and paint yellow and orange stripes down the handle.

SOCK puppets
you will need...

For Goldilocks

Sock

Wool, cut into lengths about
   36 cm (14 in)

Wool, cut into lengths about
   5 cm (2 in)

Ribbon, about 30 cm
   (12 in)

2 small buttons

2 small fabric
   circles or
   round stickers

Sewing thread

Needle

Glue

Give Goldilocks rosy cheeks made of fabric

Glue on felt ears of different shapes.

Balloons glued on make floppy ears.

Dragon has a zigzag piece of felt glued along the back of his head and neck.

Mouse has a twisted string tail and wool whiskers sewn in place.

making a sock puppet...

Goldilocks

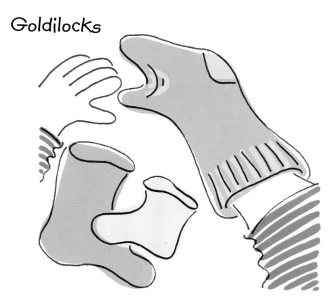

1 Put your hand in the sock with your fingertips in the toe, and the heel over your knuckles. Push the toe between your thumb and fingers to form a mouth. The heel will be the head of the puppet. Mark where the eyes will go. Take off the sock.

2 Stitch a fringe of short strands of wool to the head with a needle and thread. Lay the long strands of wool over the head, overlapping the fringe. Hang an even length down each side. Stitch to the top of the head. Plait the wool and tie with ribbon.

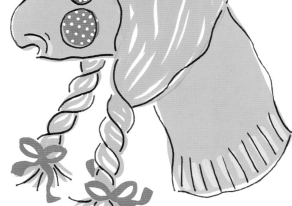

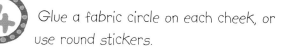

3 Sew or glue on buttons for the eyes over the markings.

4 Glue a fabric circle on each cheek, or use round stickers.

MAKE-BELIEVE
masks + headgear

Tea Party Body Masks

Painted Pasta Crowned Masks

Papier Mâché Farm Animal Masks

Googly Eyes Masks

Jungle Masks

TEA PARTY BODY masks

you will need...

For the Teapot

Thick card, about 60 cm (72 in)
   square (large cardboard box)

Thin card, about 5 x 40 cm (2 x 16 in)

Fabric, 2 strips
   about 5 x 30 cm
   (2 x 12 in)

Paints

Paintbrushes

Stapler

Scissors

Glue

Wrapping paper glued onto the card gives exciting results.

Shoulder straps may also be cut from thin card and stapled in place.

Paint a cupcake design for a younger brother or sister to wear.

Wear the lid handle like a hat.

These painted cakes look good enough to eat!

Draw a lid on the teapot with felt pen.

making a body mask...

Teapot

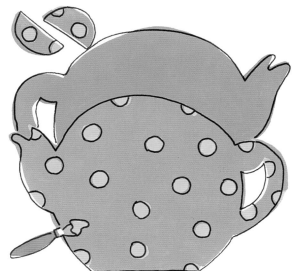

1 Cut 2 teapot shapes and one circle out of cardboard. Cut the circle in half for the lid handle.

2 Making sure you have the inner sides together, paint and decorate the outside of the teapot and lid pieces.

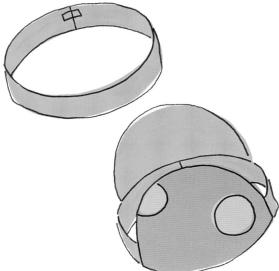

3 Staple the 2 fabric shoulder straps to the front and then the back of the teapot. Make sure you leave enough space for your head to fit between the straps.

4 For the lid handle, staple the strip of thin card into a circle to fit round your head. Glue one semicircle to the front of the circle, and one to the back. (The painted side should face outwards.) Stick tape over the staple.

PAINTED PASTA CROWNED masks

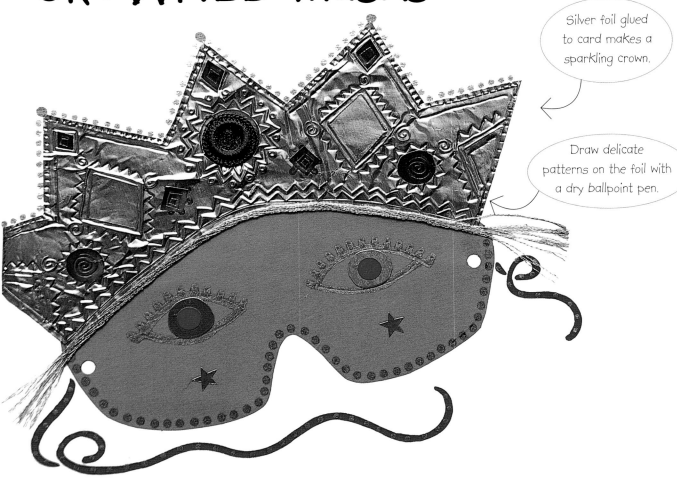

Silver foil glued to card makes a sparkling crown.

Draw delicate patterns on the foil with a dry ballpoint pen.

you will need...

Thin card, about 25 x 15 cm (10 x 6 in)
Gold card, about 25 x 15 cm (10 x 6 in)
Elastic or ribbon, about 50 cm (20 in)
2 small square stickers
Assorted pasta shapes, uncooked
Gold paint or gold marker pen
Silver paint or silver marker pen

Paintbrushes
Foil sweet wrappers
Sequins
Stickers
Hole punch
Scissors
Glue

234

making a crowned mask...

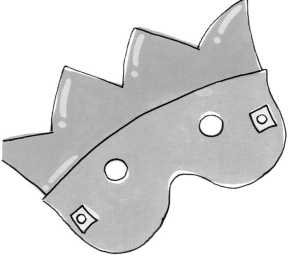

1 Cut the mask from thin card and the crown from gold card, using the pictures opposite as a guide. Glue together so that the crown overlaps the mask.

2 Cut out eye holes. Stick a sticker on each side of the mask, at the back. Punch a hole in each with the hole punch.

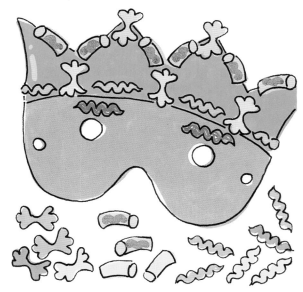

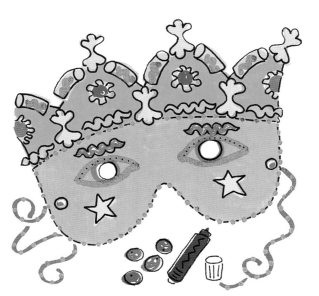

3 Paint the pasta shapes gold and silver (or use marker pens). Glue the pasta in a majestic pattern onto the crown and above the eye holes.

4 Decorate the mask and crown with sequins, foil wrappers and stickers. Add details with gold/silver pens. Knot the elastic through the holes at the sides.

PAPIER MÂCHÉ FARM ANIMAL masks

you will need...

For Buttercup the Cow

Balloon, inflated

Petroleum jelly

Newspaper, torn into strips

Newspaper, rolled up and taped to hold

Egg carton, 2-egg section

Cardboard, about 10 x 25 cm
 (4 x 10 in)

White poster paint
 or emulsion

Brown, red, orange,
 pink, yellow, green
 tissue paper,

Raffia or string, scraps

Elastic, about 50 cm
 (20 in)

Sticky tape

Scissors

Glue, diluted with water

Use pink tissue for Buttercup's tender nose and ears.

Buttercup's tail is made from a rolled newspaper.

Glue the buttercup in place where Buttercup's mouth would be.

Make Pig's nose and ears the same way as Buttercup's, but turn her ears to face downwards!

For Pig's tail, cut a curly shape from card and cover with pink tissue.

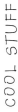

making a farm animal mask...

Buttercup

1 Cover the balloon with petroleum jelly. Dip strips of newspaper into the glue and paste about 10 layers on half the balloon. Allow to dry. (See page 245).

2 Tape on the cut egg carton nose. Cut 2 ears from card and tape in place. Paste newspaper strips over the joins. Allow to dry.

3 Pop the balloon. Trim the edges of the mask and cut holes for eyes. Paint the mask white all over.

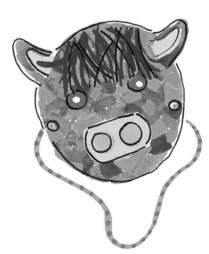

4 Tear up tissue paper, dip in diluted glue and paste layers as before, building up the colour. Allow to dry.

5 Glue on a raffia fringe. Make 2 holes on the sides of the mask. Knot elastic through the holes.

6 For the flower, paste tissue on a cardboard flower. Paste tissue on the rolled newspaper tail and tape a bundle of raffia at the end.

GOOGLY EYES masks
you will need...

For the Star Mask

Thin coloured card, about
    4 × 70 cm (1½ × 28 in)

Thin coloured card, about 15 × 10 cm
    (6 × 4 in)

Coloured tissue paper, cut into
    thin strips

2 coloured pipe cleaners

Assorted beads

Star stickers

Felt tip pens

Paper clips

Stapler

Sewing thread

Needle

Scissors

Glue

The decoration of the masks is up to you – make them as colourful as you can!

Make the purple antennae from a single pipe cleaner, folded in half, bent in a Y-shape and threaded with beads.

Use stickers to hold plumes of paper ribbon in place.

These spots have been drawn in with felt pen, but you could use spot stickers instead.

making a googly eyes mask...

Star

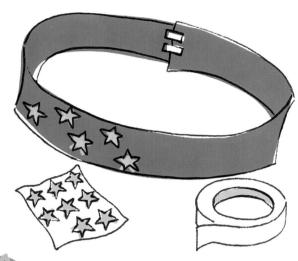

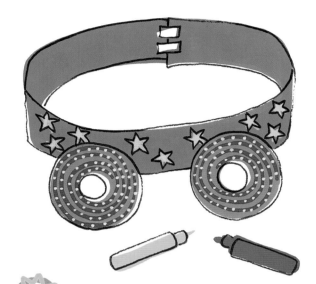

1 Make a circle with the strip of card to fit round your head. Staple. Decorate with the star stickers.

2 Cut 2 paper card circles about 7 cm (2¾ in) in diameter. Cut holes in the centre, to see out of. Draw spirals on the eyes with felt pen. Glue onto the headband.

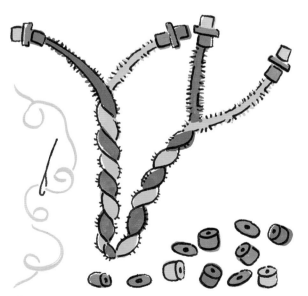

3 Fix 2 small bunches of tissue strips to paper clips. Glue the paper clips onto the sides of the headband.

4 Twist the pipe cleaners together but leave the ends free. Push beads onto the ends. Fold the pipe cleaners in half. Sew or glue the fold to the headband between the eyes.

JUNGLE MASKS

you will need...

For the Tiger

Medium-sized cardboard box

Thin card, about 10 x 20 cm (4 x 8 in)

Raffia, felt or string scraps

Elastic, about 25 cm (10 in)

Paints + paintbrushes

Felt tip pen

Craft Knife (*be careful!*)

Pencil

Parcel tape or sticky tape

Hole punch

Scissors

Glue

Ask an adult to help you cut out the eyes and nose with a craft Knife.

Glue on strips of coloured paper for a wild Lion's mane.

Glue soft felt and fabric ears in front of the mane.

Add details to the face and markings with a felt tip pen.

making a jungle mask...

Tiger

1 Cut the back and bottom off the box using scissors. Cut 2 small eye holes in the front of the box, large enough to see out of. (An adult should help you.)

2 Using the felt pen, draw in a nose and mouth, and outline the eyes. Draw the tiger markings in pencil and then paint. For extra comfort you might want to cut out the nose.

3 Cut 2 ears from thin card. Cut 2 slits in the top of the box for ears. Fold each ear 1 cm (½ in) from its bottom edge and push through the slits. Tape down the fold on the inside.

4 Glue on whiskers cut from raffia, felt or string. Unravel some string and glue on wisps to make fluffy ears. Punch a hole on each side of the box. Knot elastic at each side of the mask, so that it fits your head.

handy hints

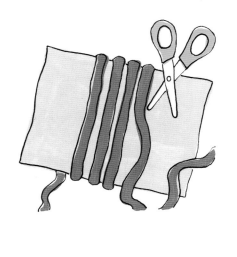

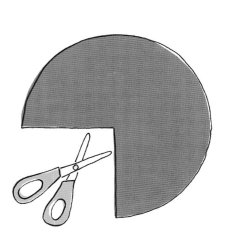

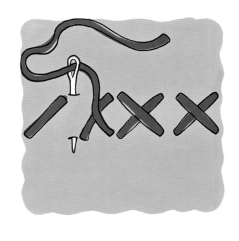

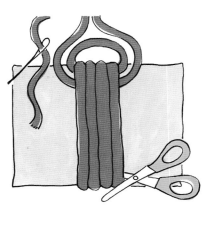

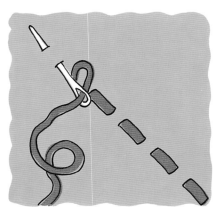

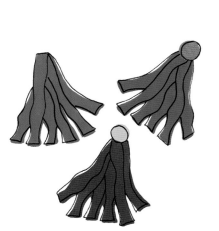

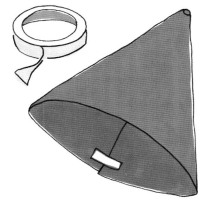

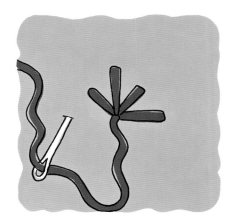

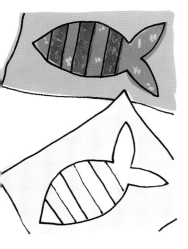

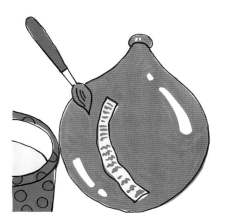

Making a Pattern

Making Papier Mâché

Making a Cone

Drying Orange Slices

Three Simple Stitches

Using Fusible Web

Making a Tassel

Making a Pompom

Making a Stencil

Making Salt Dough

243

making a pattern

① Trace the design you want (say, a rabbit) using tracing paper and a soft pencil. Make sure you hold the tracing paper steady while you trace.

② Lay the tracing paper on card, with the pencil tracing facing down. Transfer the design onto the card by drawing (or gently scribbling) over the back of the design.

③ Cut out the design from the card. This is your card pattern. The pattern faces the opposite way from the original design, but you can use either side.

④ To use the pattern, draw round it on fabric or paper and cut out the design if you need to. Using a pattern allows you to draw or cut out lots of identical designs.

making papier mâché

1 Tear newspaper into strips. Mix some glue with water, or mix up some wallpaper paste according to the instructions on the packaging.

2 Grease the balloon with petroleum jelly. Paste a strip of newspaper onto the balloon using a paintbrush and the glue or wallpaper paste.

3 Paste strips of newspaper all over the balloon, building up the layers gradually. Allow to dry for a few days. Pop the balloon. Paint and varnish the papier mâché.

Papier mâché pulp

1 For papier mâché pulp, mix newspaper strips or small pieces with dilute glue or wallpaper paste. Knead. Use as a soft clay. Dry for a few days before painting and varnishing.

HANDY HINTS

making a cone

drying orange slices

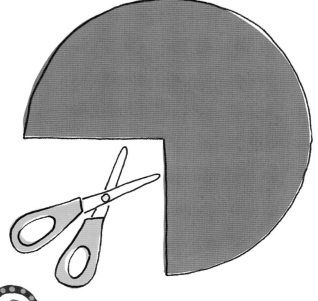

1 Cut a circle from card. The bigger the circle, the taller the cone can be. Cut out a quarter section from the circle, or simply make a cut from the edge to the centre.

1 Slice the orange thinly with a sharp knife. An adult should help you with this.

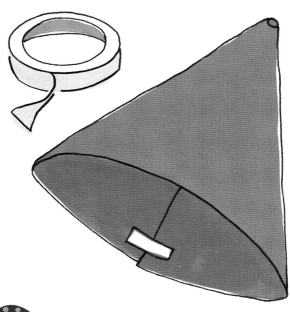

2 Overlap the edges until the circle becomes a cone. The more the edges overlap, the taller the cone will be. Tape or staple or glue the edges to hold them.

2 Put the slices on a baking tray - keep them separate. Bake in a cool oven (100°C or 200°F) until they are dry. (An adult should help you.) Do not burn them.

COOL STUFF

246

three simple stitches

Getting Started

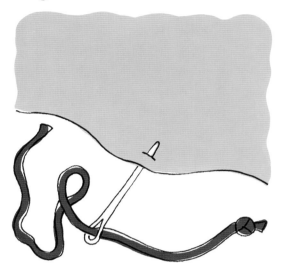

Thread the embroidery needle and knot the end of the thread. Starting from the wrong side of the fabric, push the needle through to the right side and begin stitching.

Cross Stitch

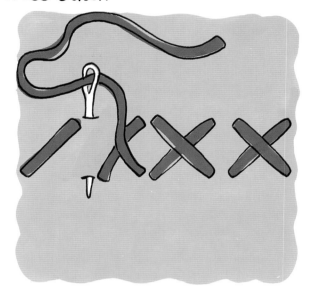

Work a row of even diagonal stitches. Then work back along the row, making diagonal stitches that cross the first row.

Running Stitch

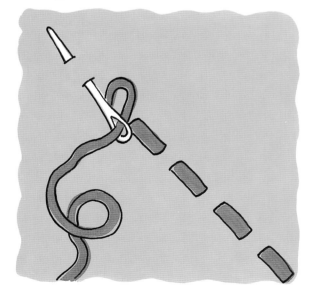

Push the needle through to the wrong side of the fabric, then bring it back through to the right side. Continue going in and out of the fabric to make a row of even stitches.

Snowflake/Star/Flower Stitch

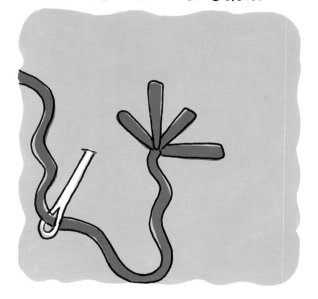

Work a group of stitches starting from a central point and stitch outwards. Bring the needle back to the centre behind the work and stitch out to make each point of the star.

using fusible web

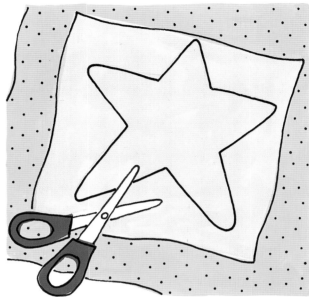

1 Iron fusible web to the wrong side of the fabric you want to use for your design. An adult should help you.

2 Cut the design you have chosen (say, a star) from the fabric using scissors.

3 Remove the paper backing from the fusible web on the star.

4 Carefully place the star, right side up, on another piece of fabric. Iron over the star to make it stick (an adult should help you).

making a tassel

Paper Tassel

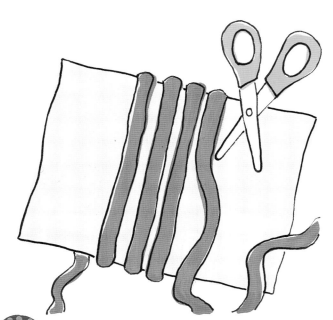

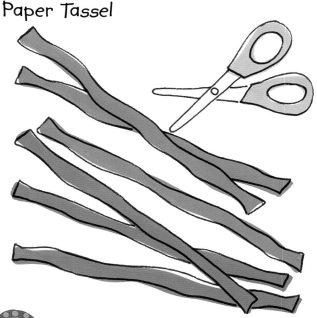

1 Wind wool, raffia or string 4 times round a rectangle of card. (The wider the card, the longer your tassel.) Cut off the extra wool.

1 To make a tissue tassel, cut tissue paper into long, narrow strips all about the same width and length.

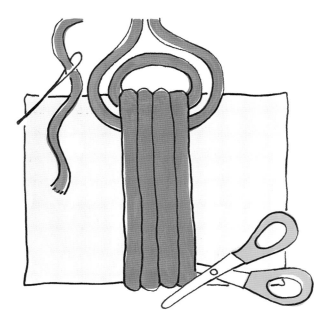

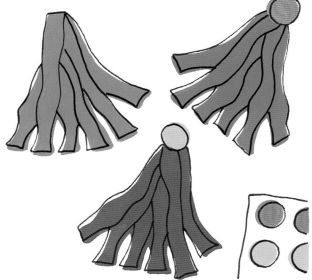

2 Push a needle threaded with wool under the wool at the top of the card. Repeat and pull tight. Make a tight knot, leaving long ends. Cut the wool along the bottom of the card.

2 Take a bunch of tissue strips and fold it in half. Simply glue the fold in place, or cover and hold with a sticker.

HANDY HINTS

249

making a pompom

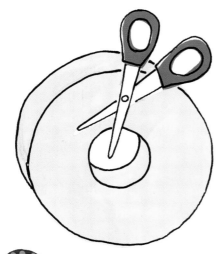

1 Draw a large circle and a smaller circle inside it on a piece of folded card, by drawing round 2 different sizes of cup or glass. Cut out the 2 identical rings.

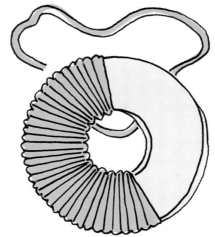

2 With the 2 rings together, wind wool around the ring. Work slowly round the ring, covering the card completely, and building up the layers of wool gradually.

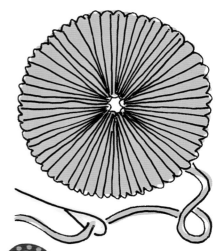

3 Keep winding the wool - the hole in the middle will start to get smaller. You will need to push the wool through the hole with a darning needle when the hole is very small.

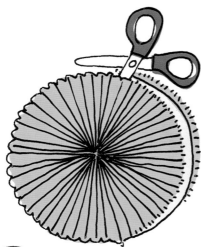

4 When the hole is blocked, use one blade of a pair of scissors to find the gap between the 2 card rings. With one blade of the scissors still in the gap, cut the wool all round the ring.

5 Slip a length of wool between the rings and tie it tightly round the bunch of wool in the middle. Leave long ends if you want to hang the pompom. Pull the rings off the wool.

6 Fluff up the pompom and make sure that the tie in the centre is hidden. For a multicoloured pompom, knot different colours of wool together and wind onto the rings as in Steps 2 and 3.

COOL STUFF

250

making a stencil

1 To make a stencil, first draw your design (say, a fish) on card. Cut out and throw away the fish shape, leaving the fish stencil.

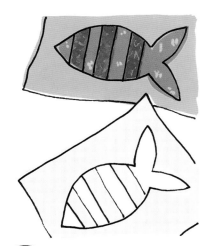

2 To make a striped fish stencil leave strips of card in the fish design when cutting out.

3 Tape the stencil to the surface you want to decorate (in this case, a plant pot), to hold it still. If it shifts, the stencil will not be clear.

4 Pour a little paint in a lid or saucer. Dip a sponge in the paint and dab it onto a paper towel to get rid of excess paint. The sponge should be almost dry. Dab the sponge on the stencil.

5 Slowly build up the colour until the stencil shape is finished. Allow the paint to dry before carefully lifting off the stencil.

6 For a 2-step stencil, like this butterfly, complete the first stencil (wings) as in Steps 3-5. Carefully tape the next stencil (body) exactly over the first stencil. Complete the second stencil.

251

making salt dough

1 Mix 3 cups of flour, a cup of salt and a drizzle of oil in a bowl. Add about a cup of water to make a soft dough. If it is sticky, add a little flour. If dry, add water.

2 Knead the dough until it comes away from the sides of the bowl. Salt dough will keep for several days if you store it in an airtight plastic bag or box.

3 Roll out the dough or mould it into the shape you need. Sprinkle flour on the work surface to stop the dough sticking. Stick pieces together with a drop of water.

4 Place the dough on a baking tray. Bake a thick piece, like a figure, at 100°C (200°F) for 2-3 hours. Bake a thin piece at 150°C (300°F) for 1½ hours.

5 Tap the back of the cooled piece - a 'thud' means it is not dried, and needs to go back in the oven; a 'ring' means it is dry. Look also for wet dough at the back.

6 When the dough is cold, it is ready to be handled. Paint the dough and add a coat of varnish to seal it.

Patterns

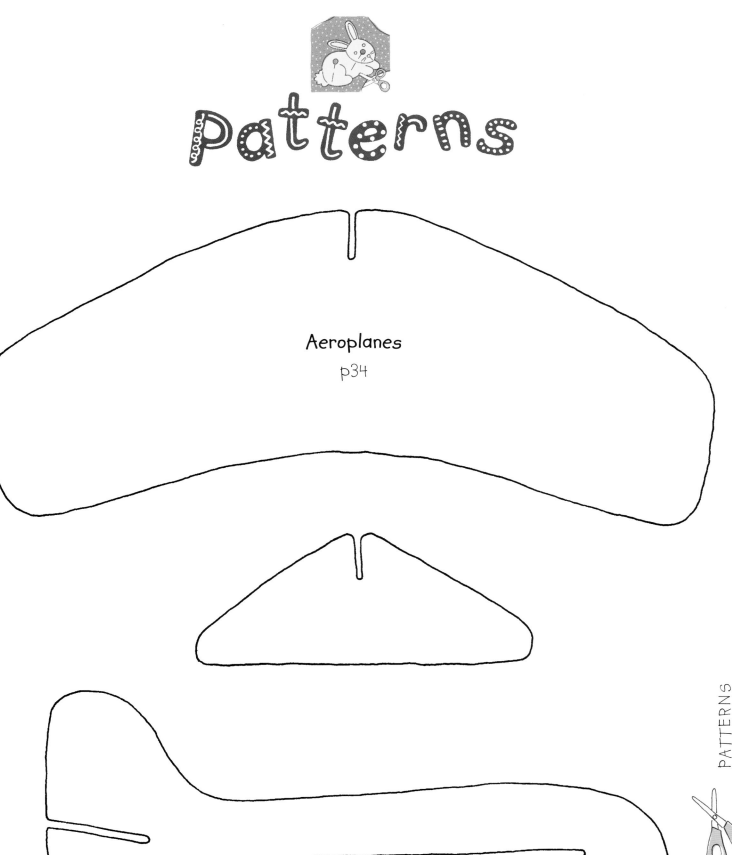

Aeroplanes

p34

Christmas Stocking

p108

index

COOL STUFF

256